Table of Content

I. Introduction

A. Overview of network security evolution
B. Importance of securing modern digital enterprises
C. Brief introduction to Secure Access Service Edge (SASE)
D. Purpose of the comparison: Why upgrading from traditional security to SASE is essential

II. Understanding Traditional Network Security

A. **Key Components of Traditional Security Models**
1. On-premises firewalls and intrusion prevention systems
2. Virtual Private Networks (VPNs) for remote access
3. Data centers as central network hubs
4. Perimeter-based security model
B. **Challenges of Traditional Network Security**
1. Increasing attack surfaces with cloud adoption and remote work
2. Complex and costly infrastructure maintenance
3. Lack of scalability and flexibility for modern workloads
4. Performance issues due to backhauling traffic through data centers
5. Security gaps in managing mobile and hybrid workforce

III. Introduction to Secure Access Service Edge (SASE)

A. Definition of SASE and how it differs from traditional models
B. Key principles behind SASE: Converging networking and security in the cloud
C. Evolution of SASE as a response to modern security challenges

IV. Core Components of SASE

A. **Software-Defined WAN (SD-WAN)** – Efficiently managing global connectivity
B. **Zero Trust Network Access (ZTNA)** – Eliminating implicit trust for better security
C. **Cloud-Delivered Firewall as a Service (FWaaS)** – Scalable and distributed firewall protection
D. **Secure Web Gateway (SWG)** – Filtering web traffic and preventing threats
E. **Cloud Access Security Broker (CASB)** – Protecting cloud applications and services
F. **Data Loss Prevention (DLP)** – Preventing unauthorized data access and leaks

V. Comparing SASE and Traditional Network Security

Feature	Traditional Network Security	SASE
Security Model	Perimeter-based	Cloud-native, zero trust
Scalability	Limited and expensive	Highly scalable and cost-effective
Remote Work Support	VPN-dependent, slow performance	Secure, direct cloud access
Performance	Backhauled traffic, high latency	Optimized with SD-WAN
Deployment	Hardware-intensive, complex	Cloud-delivered, simplified
Threat Protection	Reactive, siloed security	Proactive, integrated security services
Cost	High infrastructure and maintenance costs	Reduced operational expenses

VI. Why It's Time to Upgrade to SASE

A. **Better Security in a Cloud-First World**
- Zero Trust model for stronger access controls
- Continuous security enforcement across users, devices, and applications

B. **Enhanced Performance and User Experience**
- Direct-to-cloud connections reducing latency
- SD-WAN optimizing application performance

C. **Simplified Network and Security Management**
- Unified security and networking reducing complexity
- Centralized policy enforcement

D. **Cost Efficiency and Future-Proofing**
- Lower total cost of ownership (TCO) compared to maintaining legacy hardware
- Adaptability to future security threats and enterprise needs

VII. Implementation Considerations for SASE Adoption

A. Assessing current network and security architecture
B. Defining security and networking policies for the transition
C. Choosing the right SASE provider based on business needs
D. Phased deployment strategy for minimal disruption
E. Continuous monitoring and optimization

VIII. Conclusion

A. Recap of why traditional security is outdated
B. Summary of SASE's key advantages
C. Encouragement for organizations to evaluate and transition to SASE
D. Final thoughts on the future of network security

Foreword

In an era where digital transformation is accelerating at an unprecedented pace, the way we approach network security must evolve to keep up. Organizations are increasingly relying on cloud applications, remote workforces, and globally distributed teams, making traditional security models inadequate for modern demands. **Perimeter-based security architectures, once considered the gold standard, now struggle to protect today's highly dynamic and decentralized IT environments.**

This book, **SASE vs. Traditional Network Security: Why It's Time to Upgrade**, arrives at a crucial time when businesses are grappling with the limitations of legacy security frameworks. Traditional solutions—such as firewalls, VPNs, and data center-based security—were designed for a world where corporate applications and users resided within a clearly defined network perimeter. However, the rapid adoption of **cloud services, Software-as-a-Service (SaaS) applications, and mobile workforces** has rendered these conventional security approaches ineffective, costly, and difficult to scale.

Enter **Secure Access Service Edge (SASE)**—a modern, cloud-first security architecture that integrates **networking and security into a unified, scalable framework**. SASE is not just another incremental upgrade; it represents a fundamental shift in how security is delivered. By combining **Zero Trust Network Access (ZTNA), Secure Web Gateway (SWG), Cloud Access Security Broker (CASB), Firewall as a Service (FWaaS), and Software-Defined WAN (SD-WAN)**, SASE ensures that security is applied dynamically, regardless of where users or applications reside.

This book provides a **comprehensive comparison between traditional security models and SASE**, illustrating why organizations must **embrace a cloud native, Zero Trust approach** to stay secure in today's threat landscape. Through well-researched insights, real-world examples, and practical implementation guidance, the author makes a compelling case for why **upgrading to SASE is not just an option but a necessity**.

For IT leaders, security professionals, and decision-makers, this book serves as an essential guide to understanding how **SASE can simplify security operations, improve performance, and future-proof your organization's network security strategy**.

It's time to move beyond legacy security models. It's time to embrace SASE.

About the Author

Donald Mwase is a seasoned **Network Architect, Engineer, and Cybersecurity Consultant** with over a decade of hands-on experience in designing, securing, and optimizing complex network infrastructures. With a deep understanding of enterprise, government, and defense ICT environments, Donald Mwase has played a pivotal role in transforming legacy systems into modern, secure, and high-performing networks.

Currently serving as a **Senior Network Architect at the Cabinet Office**, Donald Mwase leads critical initiatives in **network modernization, cybersecurity strategy, and zero-trust architecture**. His expertise spans **Secure Access Service Edge (SASE), cloud networking, and advanced threat mitigation**, making him a trusted advisor in the rapidly evolving security landscape.

With an impressive portfolio of certifications, including **CCNP, CCNA Security, JNCIA-JUNOS, ITIL, and Sophos Certified Engineer**, Donald Mwase brings a wealth of knowledge in **Cisco, Juniper, Palo Alto, AWS, and enterprise encryption solutions**. His ability to anticipate and mitigate security risks has been instrumental in **fortifying enterprise networks against emerging cyber threats**.

Throughout his career, Donald Mwase has successfully:

- **Led the transformation** of government network infrastructures to **adopt SASE** for improved security and performance.
- **Implemented zero-trust security models**, reducing vulnerabilities and strengthening access controls.
- **Designed and deployed next-generation firewalls, encryption systems, and cloud security frameworks** to enhance organizational resilience.
- **Mentored and trained cybersecurity and network engineering teams**, fostering a culture of innovation and security-first thinking.

Passionate about **bridging the gap between traditional network security and future-ready solutions**, Donald Mwase is committed to helping organizations **navigate the shift from legacy security models to SASE-powered architectures**. His insights into **network security trends, risk management, and emerging technologies** make him a sought-after expert in the industry.

In **"SASE vs. Traditional Network Security: Why It's Time to Upgrade"**, Donald Mwase breaks down the limitations of legacy security models and explains why businesses must embrace **cloud-native, scalable, and adaptive security solutions** to stay ahead of evolving cyber threats.

Introduction

Overview of Network Security Evolution

Network security has undergone a profound transformation over the decades, driven by technological advancements, evolving cyber threats, and the growing need for secure digital communication. From the early days of simple firewalls to today's sophisticated cloud-based security frameworks, the evolution of network security reflects the continuous battle between security professionals and cybercriminals. Understanding this evolution provides insights into why traditional security measures are no longer sufficient in modern, highly distributed IT environments.

The Early Days: Perimeter-Based Security

In the early days of networking, security was largely focused on protecting internal systems from external threats. Organizations relied heavily on perimeter-based security, where firewalls and intrusion prevention systems (IPS) acted as the first line of defense. These security mechanisms operated on a simple principle: if you were inside the corporate network, you were trusted; if you were outside, you were not. Firewalls filtered network traffic based on predefined rules, while antivirus software protected endpoints from known malware. During this time, most business applications and data were hosted on-premises, and employees accessed corporate resources from fixed office locations. This made security relatively straightforward, as IT teams could control access through a well-defined network perimeter.

The Rise of the Internet and Remote Access Challenges

As businesses embraced the internet in the 1990s and early 2000s, network security needed to adapt to accommodate remote workers, business partners, and third-party vendors who required secure access to corporate systems. Virtual Private Networks (VPNs) emerged as a solution, allowing remote users to establish encrypted connections to corporate networks. While VPNs enhanced security for remote access, they introduced new challenges, such as performance issues and increased complexity in managing access permissions. At the same time, cyber threats grew more sophisticated, with hackers exploiting vulnerabilities in perimeter-based defenses. Worms, viruses, and Distributed Denial-of-Service (DDoS) attacks became prevalent, forcing security teams to implement more advanced intrusion detection systems (IDS) and intrusion prevention systems (IPS) to monitor and mitigate threats.

The Cloud Computing Era and the Weakening of the Network Perimeter

The rise of cloud computing in the 2010s dramatically changed the way businesses operated, shifting workloads from on-premises data centers to cloud environments. This shift weakened the traditional network perimeter, as employees, applications, and data were no longer confined to a single physical location. Organizations adopted Software-as-a-Service (SaaS) applications like Microsoft 365, Google Workspace, and Salesforce, which required security models to extend beyond traditional firewalls. Cloud security solutions such as Cloud Access Security Brokers (CASBs) and Secure Web Gateways (SWGs) were introduced to protect data stored and accessed in the cloud. However, managing security across multiple cloud providers and hybrid environments became increasingly complex, leading to the need for a more holistic, identity-centric approach to security.

The Emergence of Zero Trust and Identity-Based Security

As cyber threats continued to evolve, the concept of Zero Trust Architecture (ZTA) gained traction. Unlike traditional models that trusted users inside the corporate network, Zero Trust operates under the assumption that no user or device should be trusted by default, regardless of location. Identity and access management (IAM) solutions, multi-factor authentication (MFA), and endpoint detection and response (EDR) became critical components of security strategies. Organizations also implemented micro-segmentation, which restricted lateral movement within networks, preventing attackers from gaining access to critical systems even if they breached initial defenses. This shift marked a departure from static, perimeter-based security to a dynamic, context-aware security framework.

The Rise of SASE: A Converged Approach to Security and Networking

With remote work becoming the norm and cloud adoption accelerating, Secure Access Service Edge (SASE) emerged as the next evolution in network security. Introduced by Gartner in 2019, SASE converges networking and security into a single cloud-delivered framework, integrating technologies like Software-Defined WAN (SD-WAN), Zero Trust Network Access (ZTNA), cloud security gateways, and AI-driven threat intelligence. Unlike traditional security models that rely on central data centers, SASE enables direct-to-cloud security enforcement, reducing latency, improving performance, and providing consistent security policies regardless of user location. This approach aligns with modern digital transformation strategies, offering scalable, flexible, and cost-effective security solutions for enterprises of all sizes.

The Future of Network Security: AI, Automation, and Adaptive Threat Defense

Looking ahead, network security will continue to evolve with advancements in artificial intelligence (AI), machine learning, and automation. AI-driven security analytics can detect anomalies in real time, predicting and preventing cyber threats before they cause damage. Adaptive security frameworks will leverage behavioral analytics to assess user activity dynamically, allowing organizations to proactively respond to emerging threats. As cybersecurity threats become more sophisticated, the integration of AI-powered security orchestration and automated incident response will play a crucial role in defending against ransomware, nation-state attacks, and insider threats.

Conclusion

The evolution of network security has been a continuous journey of adaptation, driven by changing business needs and an ever-expanding threat landscape. From the early days of firewalls and VPNs to the modern adoption of SASE and Zero Trust, security frameworks have evolved to address the challenges of cloud computing, remote work, and advanced cyber threats. As businesses continue their digital transformation, adopting a security model that is agile, scalable, and intelligence-driven will be essential to protecting sensitive data and maintaining business continuity in an increasingly interconnected world.

The Importance of Securing Modern Digital Enterprises

In today's hyper-connected world, securing modern digital enterprises is more critical than ever. Organizations rely on digital technologies for daily operations, from cloud computing and remote collaboration to artificial intelligence and big data analytics. While these advancements drive innovation and efficiency, they also introduce significant security risks. Cybercriminals are constantly developing more sophisticated attacks, targeting businesses of all sizes with ransomware, data breaches, and advanced persistent threats (APTs). To protect sensitive information, maintain business continuity, and uphold customer trust, enterprises must adopt robust security strategies tailored to the evolving threat landscape.

The Expanding Attack Surface in the Digital Age

As businesses embrace cloud computing, the Internet of Things (IoT), and hybrid work environments, their attack surface expands exponentially. Unlike traditional IT infrastructures that relied on centralized security perimeters, modern enterprises operate in decentralized environments where employees, applications, and data are spread across multiple locations and devices. This shift means that security can no longer depend solely on firewalls and on-premises controls. Cybercriminals exploit this complexity by targeting cloud environments, unsecured endpoints, and remote access systems. Without comprehensive security measures, organizations are at risk of data breaches, service disruptions, and financial losses.

Rising Cyber Threats and Financial Implications

Cyberattacks have become more frequent and costly, with businesses facing financial and reputational damage from data breaches, ransomware attacks, and insider threats. According to cybersecurity reports, the average cost of a data breach has reached millions of dollars, factoring in legal fees, regulatory fines, operational downtime, and reputational harm. Ransomware attacks, where cybercriminals encrypt an organization's data and demand payment for its release, have crippled critical industries, including healthcare, finance, and government services. Additionally, cybercriminals are leveraging artificial intelligence (AI) and automation to launch more targeted and evasive attacks, making traditional security defenses inadequate.

Regulatory Compliance and Data Protection Laws

With the increasing importance of data privacy, governments and regulatory bodies worldwide have implemented strict cybersecurity laws and compliance requirements. Regulations such as the General Data Protection Regulation (GDPR), California Consumer Privacy Act (CCPA), and the Health Insurance Portability and Accountability Act (HIPAA) require enterprises to implement strong data protection measures. Failure to comply with these regulations can lead to severe financial penalties and legal consequences. Organizations must prioritize security frameworks that align with regulatory requirements, ensuring that customer data, intellectual property, and financial records remain protected from unauthorized access and misuse.

The Role of Zero Trust in Enterprise Security

To address modern security challenges, enterprises are increasingly adopting the Zero Trust security model. Unlike traditional security architectures that operate on implicit trust, Zero Trust follows a "never trust, always verify" approach. This means that every user, device, and application must continuously authenticate and validate their identity before gaining access to enterprise resources. Zero Trust Network Access (ZTNA) ensures that employees and third parties only have access to the resources they need, minimizing the risk of insider threats and lateral movement by attackers. By implementing multi-factor authentication (MFA), endpoint detection and response (EDR), and micro-segmentation, organizations can strengthen their security posture against evolving cyber threats.

Cloud Security and the Shift to Secure Access Service Edge (SASE)

As enterprises migrate their workloads to cloud environments, traditional security models struggle to keep up with dynamic and distributed infrastructures. Secure Access Service Edge (SASE) has emerged as a next-generation security framework that integrates networking and security into a cloud-delivered solution. By combining Software-Defined Wide Area Networking (SD-WAN), Zero Trust Network Access (ZTNA), Secure Web Gateway (SWG), and Cloud Access Security Broker (CASB), SASE provides enterprises with a unified security architecture. This approach reduces latency, improves performance, and ensures that security policies are consistently enforced across all users and devices, regardless of their location.

Protecting Intellectual Property and Business Continuity

For digital enterprises, intellectual property (IP) is one of the most valuable assets. Whether it's proprietary software, trade secrets, or customer databases, unauthorized access or theft of critical business information can have devastating consequences. Cyber espionage, insider threats, and nation-state attacks pose significant risks to enterprises operating in highly competitive industries. Implementing data encryption, access controls, and behavioral analytics helps organizations detect and mitigate threats before they cause irreversible damage. Additionally, security measures such as automated backup systems, disaster recovery plans, and business continuity frameworks ensure that organizations can recover quickly from cyber incidents and operational disruptions.

The Role of Artificial Intelligence and Automation in Security

Modern security threats are increasingly automated, requiring enterprises to adopt AI-driven security solutions to stay ahead of cybercriminals. Artificial intelligence (AI) and machine learning (ML) enable organizations to analyze vast amounts of security data in real-time, identifying anomalies, detecting advanced threats, and responding proactively. AI-powered threat intelligence platforms can predict attack patterns and enhance incident response by automating security workflows. Security orchestration, automation, and response (SOAR) platforms help enterprises streamline threat detection and remediation, reducing response times and minimizing human error in cybersecurity operations.

The Human Factor: Cybersecurity Awareness and Training

While technological solutions play a critical role in securing digital enterprises, human error remains one of the biggest cybersecurity vulnerabilities. Social engineering attacks, such as phishing and business email compromise (BEC), continue to exploit employees' lack of security awareness. Enterprises must invest in cybersecurity training programs to educate employees on recognizing phishing attempts, safeguarding sensitive information, and following best practices for secure digital behavior. Establishing a strong security culture within the organization is essential to preventing accidental data leaks and mitigating the risk of insider threats.

Future-Proofing Security for Digital Transformation

As enterprises continue their digital transformation journey, securing their infrastructure, applications, and data must remain a top priority. The adoption of emerging technologies such as the Internet of Things (IoT), blockchain, and 5G connectivity introduces new security challenges that require proactive risk management. Organizations must continuously assess their security posture, adopt adaptive security frameworks, and invest in cybersecurity innovations to stay resilient against future threats. By integrating security into every aspect of digital transformation, enterprises can maintain trust, drive business growth, and protect their digital assets from evolving cyber risks.

Conclusion

Securing modern digital enterprises is no longer optional—it is a business necessity. As organizations navigate a rapidly changing digital landscape, they must adopt a security-first mindset that embraces Zero Trust principles, cloud security frameworks like SASE, and AI-driven threat intelligence. Protecting data, securing remote work environments, and complying with regulatory requirements are essential for maintaining operational resilience and customer confidence. By prioritizing security, enterprises can not only defend against cyber threats but also create a competitive advantage in an increasingly digital world.

Brief Introduction to Secure Access Service Edge (SASE)

Secure Access Service Edge (SASE) is a revolutionary framework that converges network security and wide-area networking (WAN) into a unified, cloud-delivered solution. Introduced by Gartner in 2019, SASE represents a shift from traditional security models that rely on on-premises hardware to a more flexible, scalable, and cloud-native approach. As enterprises continue to embrace digital transformation, cloud computing, and remote work, the limitations of legacy security architectures become more apparent. SASE addresses these challenges by integrating key security functions such as Zero Trust Network Access (ZTNA), Cloud Access Security Broker (CASB), Secure Web Gateway (SWG), and Firewall-as-a-Service (FWaaS) into a single service that can be deployed and managed across globally distributed networks.

The Need for SASE in Modern Enterprises

Traditional network security models were designed for an era when users, applications, and data were confined to on-premises environments. Security perimeters were built around corporate data centers, and access control was based on the assumption that anything inside the network was trustworthy. However, the widespread adoption of cloud applications, Software-as-a-Service (SaaS) platforms, and remote work has rendered perimeter-based security models ineffective. Employees now access business-critical applications from various locations and devices, creating a dynamic and complex security challenge.

Cyber threats have also become more sophisticated, with attackers targeting cloud environments, endpoints, and remote access systems. Organizations that rely on traditional Virtual Private Networks (VPNs) for secure remote connectivity face issues such as poor performance, scalability limitations, and increased exposure to cyber threats. SASE addresses these challenges by providing a direct-to-cloud security model that enforces security policies at the edge, ensuring secure access regardless of the user's location.

Key Components of SASE

SASE is a holistic security and networking framework that integrates several critical technologies:

1. **Zero Trust Network Access (ZTNA)** – Unlike traditional VPNs that grant broad access to corporate networks, ZTNA ensures that users and devices are authenticated and authorized before being granted access to specific applications or services. This minimizes the risk of lateral movement by attackers within the network.
2. **Cloud Access Security Broker (CASB)** – CASB solutions provide visibility and control over cloud applications, ensuring compliance, preventing data leakage, and protecting against unauthorized access. CASB helps organizations secure SaaS applications such as Microsoft 365, Google Workspace, and Salesforce.
3. **Secure Web Gateway (SWG)** – SWG solutions protect users from web-based threats by filtering malicious content, enforcing acceptable use policies, and preventing data exfiltration. SWG is essential for organizations that need to secure employee internet access, regardless of their location.
4. **Firewall-as-a-Service (FWaaS)** – FWaaS delivers advanced firewall capabilities, including deep packet inspection, intrusion prevention, and threat intelligence, through a cloud-based model. This eliminates the need for on-premises firewalls and allows organizations to enforce consistent security policies across all locations.
5. **Software-Defined Wide Area Networking (SD-WAN)** – SD-WAN optimizes network performance by intelligently routing traffic across multiple network connections, reducing latency, and improving application performance. SD-WAN works alongside SASE's security components to ensure a seamless and secure user experience.

How SASE Improves Security and Performance

One of the most significant advantages of SASE is its ability to provide both security and network performance enhancements simultaneously. Traditional security architectures often create bottlenecks as traffic is routed through centralized data centers for inspection before reaching its final destination. This process increases latency and degrades the user experience, especially for cloud-based applications.

SASE eliminates these inefficiencies by enforcing security policies at the edge of the network, closer to the user. This reduces the need for backhauling traffic through corporate data centers and allows organizations to securely connect users directly to cloud applications. Additionally, SASE uses AI-driven threat intelligence and real-time analytics to detect and mitigate cyber threats proactively, reducing the risk of data breaches and unauthorized access.

SASE and the Future of Enterprise Security

As organizations continue to adopt hybrid work models and cloud-first strategies, SASE is expected to become the foundation of modern network security. The growing adoption of IoT devices, edge computing, and artificial intelligence will further drive the need for scalable and adaptive security solutions. By converging networking and security into a unified framework, SASE provides enterprises with the flexibility, agility, and resilience needed to thrive in today's rapidly evolving digital landscape.

In conclusion, Secure Access Service Edge (SASE) is a game-changing approach to enterprise security that addresses the shortcomings of traditional network architectures. By integrating security and networking into a cloud-native model, SASE enables organizations to enhance security, improve network performance, and support the evolving needs of a distributed workforce. As cyber threats become more sophisticated and businesses continue their digital transformation journey, adopting SASE will be essential for ensuring secure and seamless connectivity across modern enterprise environments.

Purpose of the Comparison: Why Upgrading from Traditional Security to SASE Is Essential

As enterprises undergo digital transformation, traditional security architectures are struggling to keep up with evolving business needs and cyber threats. Legacy security models were designed for a time when employees worked within corporate offices, applications resided in on-premises data centers, and security perimeters were well-defined. However, with the rapid adoption of cloud computing, remote work, and mobile access, these traditional security approaches have become obsolete.

The shift from traditional network security to Secure Access Service Edge (SASE) is not just a trend but a necessity for modern enterprises. Businesses must ensure secure, seamless, and efficient access to applications and data, regardless of the user's location or the device they are using. SASE integrates networking and security into a unified cloud-delivered model, overcoming the inefficiencies and vulnerabilities of legacy security frameworks. This comparison highlights why upgrading from traditional security to SASE is crucial for organizations looking to protect their data, improve network performance, and support a dynamic workforce.

Traditional Security Struggles to Protect Distributed Workforces

In the past, enterprises relied on perimeter-based security models that centralized security controls in on-premises data centers. Firewalls, Virtual Private Networks (VPNs), and Intrusion Prevention Systems (IPS) were deployed to monitor and protect internal networks. However, these traditional security measures assume that all users and applications operate within a fixed perimeter.

Today, employees access corporate resources from various locations, including home offices, coworking spaces, and public networks. This decentralization has created significant security gaps, as traditional security tools were not designed to protect users and devices outside the corporate network. VPNs, once a staple for remote work, introduce latency, scalability challenges, and security risks, such as credential theft and unauthorized access. In contrast, SASE provides a more modern approach by enforcing security policies at the edge, ensuring that users and devices are protected regardless of where they connect.

The Growing Complexity of Cyber Threats Demands a Stronger Security Framework

Cyber threats have evolved beyond basic malware and phishing attacks. Organizations now face sophisticated ransomware, supply chain attacks, insider threats, and nation-state cyberattacks. Traditional security architectures, which rely on static rules and signature-based threat detection, are no longer effective in mitigating these advanced threats.

SASE integrates AI-driven threat intelligence, real-time analytics, and Zero Trust Network Access (ZTNA) to provide continuous verification of users and devices. Unlike traditional security models that grant excessive access based on static rules, SASE enforces strict access controls based on user identity, device posture, and risk levels. This dynamic and adaptive security approach significantly reduces the attack surface and prevents lateral movement by cybercriminals within the network.

Cloud Adoption Requires a Cloud-Native Security Model

Enterprises are rapidly migrating their workloads to the cloud, leveraging SaaS applications like Microsoft 365, Salesforce, and Google Workspace. However, traditional security architectures force cloud traffic to be routed through on-premises data centers for security inspection, creating performance bottlenecks and inefficiencies. This approach not only slows down application performance but also increases operational complexity for IT teams.

SASE eliminates the need for backhauling traffic through corporate data centers by applying security policies directly in the cloud. With integrated components like Cloud Access Security Broker (CASB), Secure Web Gateway (SWG), and Firewall-as-a-Service (FWaaS), SASE ensures that users securely connect to cloud applications without performance degradation. This direct-to-cloud approach enhances user experience, reduces latency, and optimizes network efficiency.

Zero Trust Security vs. Implicit Trust in Traditional Networks

Traditional security models often operate on implicit trust, assuming that users and devices inside the corporate network are inherently safe. This outdated approach increases the risk of insider threats, unauthorized access, and data breaches. Once an attacker gains access to the internal network, they can move laterally and compromise critical assets with little resistance.

SASE adopts a Zero Trust security model, enforcing a "never trust, always verify" principle. This means that every access request is authenticated, authorized, and continuously monitored, regardless of whether the user is inside or outside the corporate network. By implementing Zero Trust Network Access (ZTNA) within SASE, enterprises can prevent unauthorized access, reduce insider threats, and ensure compliance with security policies.

Cost and Operational Efficiency: Reducing IT Overhead

Managing traditional security infrastructures is costly and resource-intensive. Enterprises must maintain multiple security appliances, configure complex network policies, and continuously update security patches. Additionally, as organizations expand, they must invest in additional hardware and network upgrades to support growing bandwidth demands.

SASE simplifies security operations by consolidating multiple security functions into a cloud-delivered model. This reduces the need for expensive on-premises hardware, lowers maintenance costs, and enables IT teams to focus on strategic security initiatives rather than routine administrative tasks. The scalability of SASE allows businesses to easily adapt to changing demands without investing in costly infrastructure upgrades.

Regulatory Compliance and Data Protection

With increasing data privacy regulations such as GDPR, CCPA, and HIPAA, enterprises must implement strict security controls to protect sensitive information. Traditional security models often struggle with compliance due to fragmented security architectures and inconsistent policy enforcement across different locations.

SASE provides centralized visibility and control over security policies, ensuring that compliance requirements are met across the entire network. Integrated security features such as data loss prevention (DLP), encryption, and cloud security monitoring help organizations safeguard sensitive data and prevent regulatory violations. By adopting SASE, enterprises can achieve compliance more effectively while reducing the risk of data breaches and legal penalties.

Future-Proofing Security for the Digital Age

As organizations embrace emerging technologies like IoT, edge computing, and 5G networks, security requirements will continue to evolve. Traditional security models lack the flexibility to support these innovations, creating security gaps that attackers can exploit.

SASE is designed to be future-proof, offering a flexible and scalable security framework that adapts to new business needs and technological advancements. By integrating AI-driven security analytics, automation, and machine learning, SASE enables organizations to stay ahead of emerging threats and proactively mitigate security risks.

Conclusion: The Urgency of Upgrading to SASE

The transition from traditional security to SASE is no longer optional—it is essential for businesses to remain secure, agile, and competitive in today's digital landscape. Legacy security architectures are incapable of protecting modern enterprises from evolving cyber threats, cloud-based operations, and a remote workforce. SASE provides a comprehensive, cloud-native solution that enhances security, improves network performance, and reduces operational complexity.

Organizations that fail to upgrade their security frameworks risk falling behind in an increasingly hostile cyber environment. By adopting SASE, enterprises can ensure that security is seamlessly integrated into their digital transformation journey, enabling secure and efficient access to applications and data from anywhere in the world. Now is the time to upgrade, strengthen security postures, and embrace the future of network security with SASE.

On-Premise Firewalls and Intrusion Prevention Systems: Strengths and Limitations

On-premise firewalls and intrusion prevention systems (IPS) have long been fundamental components of enterprise network security. These solutions provide essential protection against cyber threats by monitoring, filtering, and blocking malicious traffic before it can infiltrate internal networks. While these technologies have been effective in traditional IT environments, the shift toward cloud computing, remote work, and evolving cyber threats has exposed their limitations.

The Role of On-Premise Firewalls in Network Security

Firewalls serve as the first line of defense in network security by controlling traffic between trusted internal networks and untrusted external networks, such as the internet. On-premise firewalls are hardware or software solutions deployed within an organization's data center to enforce security policies. They analyze incoming and outgoing traffic based on predefined rules, allowing or blocking connections based on factors like IP addresses, port numbers, and protocols.

Early firewalls primarily functioned as packet filters, examining the header information of network packets to determine whether they should be forwarded or dropped. However, as cyber threats became more sophisticated, firewalls evolved to include more advanced capabilities such as stateful inspection, deep packet inspection (DPI), and application-layer filtering. Modern next-generation firewalls (NGFWs) integrate additional security functions, including malware detection, intrusion prevention, and web filtering, to provide more comprehensive protection.

Intrusion Prevention Systems (IPS): Enhancing Threat Detection

While firewalls primarily focus on controlling traffic flow, intrusion prevention systems (IPS) actively monitor network traffic for signs of cyberattacks and unauthorized activities. An IPS operates by analyzing network packets and identifying known attack patterns, suspicious behavior, or policy violations. If a threat is detected, the IPS can take immediate action, such as blocking the malicious traffic, alerting security teams, or terminating a compromised session.

Intrusion prevention systems use signature-based detection to recognize known threats, anomaly-based detection to identify deviations from normal behavior, and heuristic analysis to predict and block new attack methods. Many enterprises deploy IPS solutions alongside firewalls to create a multi-layered security defense that can detect and prevent both known and emerging threats.

Strengths of On-Premise Firewalls and IPS

Despite the rise of cloud-based security solutions, on-premise firewalls and IPS still offer several advantages:

1. **Granular Control and Customization** – Organizations can configure firewalls and IPS policies to meet specific security requirements, ensuring that only authorized traffic is allowed while blocking unwanted or malicious activity.
2. **Low Latency and High Performance** – On-premise firewalls process traffic within the local network, reducing latency compared to cloud-based security solutions that may require traffic to be routed through remote data centers for inspection.
3. **Data Sovereignty and Compliance** – Some industries, such as healthcare and finance, require strict data privacy and regulatory compliance. On-premise security solutions provide organizations with full control over their data, reducing concerns about third-party cloud providers accessing sensitive information.
4. **Protection for Legacy Systems** – Many enterprises still rely on legacy applications and systems that are not designed for cloud environments. On-premise firewalls and IPS can help secure these critical assets by enforcing strict access controls and monitoring network traffic.

Limitations of On-Premise Firewalls and IPS in Modern IT Environments

While on-premise firewalls and IPS solutions have been essential for securing traditional networks, they face significant challenges in today's cloud-first, remote-work-driven landscape:

1. **Lack of Cloud Visibility and Control** – As organizations migrate applications and workloads to the cloud, on-premise security solutions struggle to provide adequate visibility and control over cloud traffic. Traditional firewalls are designed to protect network

perimeters, but cloud environments often operate without a clearly defined perimeter, making it difficult for on-premise solutions to enforce security policies effectively.

2. **Scalability Issues** – On-premise security solutions require significant investment in hardware and maintenance. As organizations grow and expand their network infrastructure, scaling on-premise firewalls and IPS can become costly and complex. Cloud-based security models, such as Secure Access Service Edge (SASE), offer a more scalable and flexible approach by providing security as a service.

3. **Remote Work Challenges** – The widespread adoption of remote work has rendered traditional perimeter-based security models insufficient. Employees connect to corporate networks from various locations and devices, often using unsecured public Wi-Fi networks. VPNs, which are commonly used alongside on-premise firewalls, introduce performance bottlenecks and increase security risks, as compromised VPN credentials can be exploited by attackers.

4. **Limited Threat Intelligence and Response Capabilities** – On-premise firewalls and IPS rely on predefined rules and static signatures to detect threats. However, modern cyber threats are increasingly sophisticated, leveraging advanced evasion techniques and zero-day exploits. Cloud-based security solutions benefit from AI-driven threat intelligence and real-time analytics, enabling organizations to detect and respond to threats more effectively.

5. **High Maintenance and Operational Costs** – Maintaining on-premise firewalls and IPS solutions requires dedicated IT personnel to monitor, update, and configure security policies regularly. As cyber threats evolve, security teams must constantly update signature databases and firewall rules to stay ahead of new attack methods. Cloud-based security solutions automate these processes, reducing the burden on IT teams.

The Shift Toward Cloud-Native Security Models

To address the limitations of on-premise firewalls and IPS, many organizations are adopting cloud-native security models such as SASE and Zero Trust Network Access (ZTNA). These modern security frameworks integrate networking and security functions into a unified, cloud-delivered solution that provides consistent protection across all users, devices, and locations.

With cloud-based security solutions, organizations can enforce security policies at the edge of the network, reducing latency and improving performance. AI-driven threat detection and machine learning algorithms enhance security by identifying anomalies in real time and adapting to evolving cyber threats. Additionally, cloud-based security models support Zero Trust principles, ensuring that all access requests are continuously authenticated and monitored.

Conclusion: The Future of Network Security

On-premise firewalls and intrusion prevention systems have played a crucial role in protecting enterprise networks for decades. However, as businesses transition to cloud environments, remote work, and mobile-first operations, traditional security architectures face growing challenges. While on-premise solutions still offer benefits in certain scenarios, they are no longer sufficient as standalone security measures in modern IT environments.

The shift toward cloud-native security models like SASE, ZTNA, and Firewall-as-a-Service (FWaaS) reflects the need for more scalable, flexible, and intelligent security frameworks. Organizations that rely solely on on-premise firewalls and IPS risk falling behind in cybersecurity posture, leaving themselves vulnerable to evolving threats. By embracing modern security solutions, businesses can ensure robust protection, improve operational efficiency, and support the dynamic needs of today's digital enterprises.

Virtual Private Networks (VPNs) for Remote Access: Strengths, Limitations, and the Future

In an era where remote work, cloud computing, and mobile connectivity have become the norm, securing remote access to corporate resources is more critical than ever. Virtual Private Networks (VPNs) have long been the go-to solution for enabling secure remote access, providing encrypted tunnels between users and enterprise networks. While VPNs have played a crucial role in securing remote connectivity, their limitations in scalability, security, and performance have become increasingly apparent in today's rapidly evolving digital landscape.

How VPNs Work: The Basics of Secure Remote Connectivity

A Virtual Private Network (VPN) is a technology that establishes a secure, encrypted connection between a user's device and a private network over a public network such as the internet. VPNs create a "tunnel" that protects data from interception, ensuring confidentiality and integrity while allowing remote users to access internal corporate resources as if they were physically on-site.

VPNs operate using various protocols, such as:

1. **Internet Protocol Security (IPSec):** Provides encryption and authentication for IP traffic, commonly used for site-to-site and remote access VPNs.
2. **Secure Sockets Layer/Transport Layer Security (SSL/TLS):** Encrypts traffic between the user's browser and the VPN server, often used in web-based remote access VPNs.
3. **Point-to-Point Tunneling Protocol (PPTP):** One of the oldest VPN protocols, but considered less secure due to vulnerabilities.
4. **WireGuard:** A modern, high-performance VPN protocol that provides strong security with minimal overhead.

VPNs can be categorized into two main types:

- **Remote Access VPNs:** Used by individual employees to securely connect to a corporate network from remote locations.
- **Site-to-Site VPNs:** Used to securely connect entire office locations or branch networks over the internet.

While VPNs have been instrumental in enabling remote work and protecting sensitive data, they also come with challenges that organizations must consider.

Advantages of VPNs for Remote Access

VPNs have been widely adopted due to their ability to provide secure and reliable remote access. Key benefits include:

1. **Encryption of Data Traffic:** VPNs use strong encryption algorithms to protect sensitive corporate data from cyber threats, ensuring that attackers cannot intercept communications.
2. **Secure Access to Internal Resources:** Employees working remotely can securely access internal applications, databases, and file servers as if they were within the corporate network.
3. **Bypassing Geo-Restrictions and Firewalls:** VPNs allow users to access services that may be restricted based on geographic location, providing greater flexibility for remote work.
4. **Cost-Effective Security Solution:** Compared to other advanced security solutions, VPNs offer a relatively affordable way to secure remote connections.
5. **Support for Public Wi-Fi Security:** When employees use public Wi-Fi in coffee shops, airports, or hotels, VPNs help protect against eavesdropping and man-in-the-middle attacks.

Despite these advantages, VPNs also come with significant limitations, particularly in large-scale remote work environments.

Challenges and Limitations of VPNs

While VPNs have been a staple in remote access security, they have several drawbacks that make them less suitable for modern enterprise security needs:

1. **Scalability Issues:** Traditional VPNs struggle to support large numbers of remote users simultaneously. Organizations often experience performance bottlenecks, slow connections, and increased latency when thousands of employees connect at once.
2. **Performance Degradation:** VPN traffic is typically routed through a central corporate data center, which can cause significant slowdowns when employees are spread across multiple geographic locations. High-bandwidth applications, such as video conferencing and cloud-based collaboration tools, often suffer from poor performance.
3. **Security Risks with Compromised Credentials:** VPNs rely heavily on username-password authentication, making them vulnerable to credential theft. If an attacker gains access to a user's VPN credentials, they can infiltrate the corporate network undetected.
4. **Lack of Granular Access Control:** Traditional VPNs grant users broad access to corporate networks once authenticated. This "all-or-nothing" approach increases the risk of insider threats and lateral movement by attackers within the network.
5. **Complex Management and Maintenance:** IT teams must continuously update and configure VPN servers, manage user credentials, and troubleshoot connectivity issues, making VPN management time-consuming.
6. **Incompatibility with Cloud-Based Environments:** VPNs were originally designed for on-premise networks. As organizations move applications and data to the cloud, VPNs often struggle to provide seamless and secure access to cloud-based resources.

Given these limitations, enterprises are increasingly looking for more modern solutions to secure remote access.

The Rise of Zero Trust and SASE as VPN Alternatives

As organizations recognize the drawbacks of traditional VPNs, many are shifting towards **Zero Trust Network Access (ZTNA)** and **Secure Access Service Edge (SASE)** models. These frameworks provide a more flexible, scalable, and secure alternative to VPN-based remote access.

1. **Zero Trust Network Access (ZTNA):** Unlike VPNs, which implicitly trust authenticated users, ZTNA operates on the principle of "never trust, always verify." It grants users access to specific applications rather than the entire network, reducing attack surfaces and preventing lateral movement by attackers.
2. **Secure Access Service Edge (SASE):** SASE integrates networking and security functions into a cloud-delivered service, offering **identity-based access control, real-time threat detection, and optimized performance**. It eliminates the need for traditional VPN backhauling by securing connections directly at the cloud edge.

SASE solutions leverage cloud-based **Firewall-as-a-Service (FWaaS), Secure Web Gateways (SWG), Cloud Access Security Brokers (CASB), and Zero Trust principles** to provide **more dynamic, policy-driven remote access security** than VPNs.

Why Organizations Are Moving Away from VPNs

Many organizations are now prioritizing **VPN alternatives** due to:

1. **The Rise of Cloud-Based Applications:** With SaaS applications like Microsoft 365, Google Workspace, and cloud storage services, employees need direct access to cloud resources without routing traffic through a centralized VPN.
2. **Work-From-Anywhere Requirements:** The traditional office-centric network model is no longer viable. Employees now connect from various locations, requiring security models that provide **adaptive, identity-based access**.
3. **Enhanced Security Against Cyber Threats:** Ransomware, phishing, and credential-stuffing attacks have made VPNs a primary attack vector. **ZTNA and SASE minimize the risk of unauthorized access and data breaches.**
4. **Operational Efficiency:** Cloud-based security solutions **reduce IT overhead, simplify management, and improve user experience** by eliminating VPN-related performance issues.

Conclusion: The Future of Secure Remote Access

Virtual Private Networks (VPNs) have been a crucial part of enterprise security for decades, providing encrypted remote access to corporate networks. However, their scalability limitations, security risks, and performance challenges have led organizations to explore more advanced alternatives.

Zero Trust Network Access (ZTNA) and Secure Access Service Edge (SASE) represent the next generation of remote access security, providing more granular, cloud-native, and identity-based security models. As enterprises continue their digital transformation journey, adopting these modern security frameworks will be critical to ensuring **seamless, secure, and efficient remote access for a distributed workforce.**

While VPNs may still have a role in specific use cases, **the shift toward Zero Trust and cloud-delivered security architectures is inevitable**—paving the way for a more secure, scalable, and resilient approach to remote work security.

Data Centers as Central Network Hubs: The Backbone of Digital Infrastructure

Data centers serve as the **central nerve centers** of modern network architecture, providing the essential infrastructure required for data storage, computing, and networking. They act as the foundation for enterprises, cloud service providers, and digital ecosystems, ensuring seamless connectivity, security, and performance for businesses and consumers alike. As technology evolves, the role of data centers is shifting from traditional on-premise infrastructure to hybrid and cloud-based architectures, making them more critical than ever.

The Role of Data Centers in Network Architecture

A data center is a **facility that houses computing resources, networking equipment, storage systems, and security solutions** to manage and process vast amounts of data. These facilities are designed to provide **high availability, redundancy, and security**, ensuring that businesses can operate without interruptions.

As central network hubs, data centers facilitate:

- **Data Processing and Storage:** Organizations rely on data centers to store and process mission-critical data. Large enterprises, financial institutions, and healthcare providers require robust data storage solutions to manage sensitive information.
- **Enterprise Connectivity:** Data centers enable seamless communication between employees, customers, and partners by managing network traffic and providing secure access to business applications.
- **Cloud Integration:** Modern data centers support hybrid and multi-cloud environments, allowing businesses to leverage public and private cloud resources for **scalability, flexibility, and cost-efficiency**.
- **Disaster Recovery and Business Continuity:** Redundant infrastructure and failover mechanisms ensure that businesses can recover quickly in the event of hardware failures, cyberattacks, or natural disasters.

By acting as the **core hub** for data transmission and resource management, data centers play a crucial role in ensuring high-speed, secure, and reliable digital operations.

Types of Data Centers and Their Evolving Role

The evolution of network security and cloud computing has led to different types of data centers, each designed to cater to specific business needs. These include:

1. **Enterprise Data Centers:** Privately owned and operated by large organizations, these facilities provide on-premise control over data and security but require significant investment in maintenance and infrastructure.
2. **Colocation Data Centers:** Businesses lease space within a third-party facility, benefiting from shared infrastructure, security, and management without the cost of building their own data centers.
3. **Cloud Data Centers:** Operated by cloud service providers (e.g., AWS, Microsoft Azure, Google Cloud), these facilities enable businesses to access **on-demand computing power and storage without physical infrastructure**.
4. **Edge Data Centers:** Small, localized facilities placed closer to end-users to reduce latency, improve performance, and support emerging technologies such as **5G, IoT, and AI-driven applications**.

The shift toward **hybrid cloud architectures** has transformed traditional data centers into **hyper-connected environments** that seamlessly integrate on-premise, colocation, and cloud-based resources.

Data Centers as the Core of Enterprise Security

As central network hubs, data centers also play a **pivotal role in cybersecurity**. Given the increasing frequency of **cyber threats such as ransomware, DDoS attacks, and insider threats**, organizations must ensure their data centers are fortified with **advanced security measures**:

- **Firewalls and Intrusion Prevention Systems (IPS):** These solutions monitor and filter incoming traffic to prevent unauthorized access and mitigate cyberattacks.
- **Zero Trust Architecture (ZTA):** Data centers are adopting Zero Trust principles to enforce **strict identity verification and least-privilege access controls**.
- **End-to-End Encryption:** Secure data transmission between data centers, cloud environments, and remote users ensures that sensitive information remains protected.
- **Redundant Backup Systems:** Disaster recovery solutions, such as geo-redundancy and automated failover, prevent **data loss and downtime** in case of disruptions.

By implementing **multi-layered security frameworks**, data centers help protect organizations from **evolving cyber threats** while ensuring **continuous business operations**.

Network Performance and Optimization in Data Centers

Modern data centers are designed to **optimize network performance** by implementing high-speed interconnectivity, automation, and software-defined networking (SDN). Key innovations that improve **data center efficiency** include:

1. **Software-Defined Networking (SDN):** SDN decouples network management from physical hardware, enabling **dynamic traffic routing, improved security policies, and automation**.

2. **Software-Defined Wide Area Networking (SD-WAN):** This technology optimizes **multi-site connectivity** by dynamically selecting the best network paths, reducing **latency and congestion**.
3. **Load Balancing and Traffic Distribution:** Data centers deploy **intelligent load balancers** to distribute traffic evenly, ensuring optimal performance and preventing bottlenecks.
4. **Content Delivery Networks (CDNs):** CDNs cache content at edge locations, reducing latency and improving user experience for streaming services, gaming, and web applications.

With these **cutting-edge network optimizations**, data centers continue to **enhance operational efficiency, scalability, and cost-effectiveness** for businesses worldwide.

Challenges and Future Trends in Data Centers

Despite their critical role, data centers face several challenges as businesses demand **greater agility, security, and sustainability**:

- **Increasing Energy Consumption:** Data centers require massive amounts of power to operate, leading to growing concerns about **energy efficiency and environmental impact**. Organizations are investing in **green data centers** that leverage renewable energy and AI-driven power optimization.
- **Cybersecurity Threats:** As cyber threats become more sophisticated, data centers must continuously evolve their security strategies to **prevent breaches and data leaks**.
- **Cloud Migration and Hybrid IT Complexity:** Businesses are increasingly adopting **hybrid and multi-cloud strategies**, requiring seamless integration between **on-premise data centers and cloud platforms**.
- **5G and Edge Computing Integration:** The rise of **5G networks and edge computing** is reshaping data center architecture, requiring more localized data processing to **reduce latency and enhance real-time applications**.

The future of data centers lies in **automation, AI-driven management, and software-defined architectures**, allowing businesses to achieve **unparalleled scalability, security, and agility**.

Conclusion: The Enduring Role of Data Centers in the Digital Age

Data centers remain the **foundation of global digital infrastructure**, providing the computing power, security, and network connectivity required for businesses to thrive. As the demand for **cloud services, remote work, and real-time applications** grows, data centers will continue to evolve into **highly automated, secure, and sustainable network hubs**.

From **enterprise IT environments to global hyperscale cloud providers**, data centers will **remain indispensable** for **powering innovation, enabling digital transformation, and securing mission-critical operations** in an increasingly interconnected world.

Perimeter-Based Security Model: The Traditional Approach to Network Protection

The **perimeter-based security model** has long been the foundation of enterprise cybersecurity, designed to protect internal networks by establishing a clear boundary between trusted and untrusted environments. This model operates under the assumption that **everything inside the corporate network is safe, while external traffic is potentially malicious**. Security tools such as **firewalls, intrusion prevention systems (IPS), and virtual private networks (VPNs)** are deployed at the network's perimeter to inspect and filter traffic before granting access to internal resources.

For decades, this model has been effective in safeguarding enterprise infrastructure, particularly when most business operations were confined to **on-premise data centers and localized corporate networks**. However, with the rise of **cloud computing, remote work, and increasingly sophisticated cyber threats**, perimeter-based security is being challenged, requiring organizations to rethink their cybersecurity strategies.

How the Perimeter-Based Security Model Works

At its core, the perimeter-based security model is akin to a **castle-and-moat** approach, where strong defenses (such as firewalls and access controls) are built around an organization's IT environment to **block unauthorized external access** while allowing trusted users inside to operate freely. Key components of this model include:

- **Firewalls:** The first line of defense, filtering incoming and outgoing traffic based on predefined rules to prevent unauthorized access.
- **Intrusion Detection and Prevention Systems (IDS/IPS):** These tools monitor network traffic for suspicious activity and can automatically block potential threats.
- **VPNs (Virtual Private Networks):** Secure encrypted tunnels that allow remote users to access the internal network while maintaining confidentiality.
- **Demilitarized Zones (DMZs):** Segmented network areas that expose certain services (such as web servers or email gateways) to external users while keeping core systems protected.
- **Access Control Lists (ACLs):** Rules that specify which users and devices can interact with specific resources inside the network.

By enforcing strict **entry points** into the network, organizations using the perimeter-based security model can create a well-guarded infrastructure where only authenticated traffic is allowed through.

Strengths of the Perimeter-Based Security Model

Despite its growing limitations, the perimeter-based security model has several advantages that have made it a preferred approach for organizations with well-defined network boundaries. Some of its key strengths include:

1. **Simplicity and Familiarity:** IT teams have relied on perimeter-based security for years, making it **easy to deploy, manage, and maintain** with existing security tools.
2. **Centralized Control:** By placing security controls at the perimeter, organizations can monitor and enforce **security policies across the entire network** from a single location.
3. **Scalability for On-Premise Infrastructure:** Traditional businesses with **on-premise data centers and limited remote access** can effectively protect their internal assets with perimeter-based defenses.
4. **Protection Against External Threats:** Firewalls and IPS systems help **block incoming attacks, such as malware, DDoS attacks, and unauthorized access attempts**.

For businesses with **fixed infrastructure and limited exposure to external networks**, this model can still provide effective security when implemented with strong policies and updated threat intelligence.

Challenges and Limitations of Perimeter-Based Security

While perimeter-based security has been effective in the past, modern cybersecurity challenges have exposed significant weaknesses in this approach. The most critical limitations include:

1. **Assumption of Trust Within the Network:** The model operates under the belief that **internal users and devices are inherently trustworthy**, which is no longer valid due to insider threats, compromised accounts, and lateral movement by attackers.
2. **Lack of Adaptability to Cloud and Remote Work:** With the rise of **cloud computing, Software-as-a-Service (SaaS), and remote work**, users and devices operate outside the traditional perimeter, making **network-based security less effective**.
3. **Vulnerabilities from VPN-Based Access:** VPNs, a common method to extend perimeter-based security to remote users, **introduce security risks** such as credential theft, poor access controls, and unmonitored lateral movement.
4. **Inability to Defend Against Modern Attacks: Advanced persistent threats (APTs), phishing, and ransomware** can bypass perimeter defenses by gaining access through compromised credentials or vulnerabilities in endpoint devices.
5. **High Operational Costs and Complexity:** As organizations expand, **managing multiple firewalls, VPN configurations, and security appliances** becomes increasingly complex and costly.

These limitations have led many organizations to **move beyond perimeter-based security** toward **zero-trust and cloud-native security models** that offer **stronger, more adaptive protection** against today's cyber threats.

The Shift from Perimeter Security to Zero Trust and SASE

To address the shortcomings of perimeter-based security, enterprises are increasingly adopting **Zero Trust Architecture (ZTA) and Secure Access Service Edge (SASE)** as modern alternatives. These models focus on:

- **Identity-Based Access:** Instead of assuming trust based on location, access is granted based on strict authentication and authorization rules, such as **multi-factor authentication (MFA) and role-based access control (RBAC).**
- **Micro-Segmentation:** Internal networks are broken into smaller, isolated segments to prevent attackers from moving laterally if they breach one part of the system.
- **Continuous Monitoring and Threat Detection:** Security policies dynamically adjust based on real-time analytics, behavioral patterns, and emerging threats.
- **Cloud-Native Security:** Security is integrated **directly into cloud services**, protecting users regardless of their location while eliminating the need for traditional perimeter defenses.

By adopting **Zero Trust and SASE**, organizations can ensure **stronger security postures**, particularly in environments where employees, devices, and workloads are distributed **beyond traditional corporate perimeters**.

Conclusion: The Declining Relevance of Perimeter-Based Security

While the perimeter-based security model has been a **cornerstone of enterprise cybersecurity for decades**, the rapid shift toward **cloud computing, remote work, and sophisticated cyber threats** has rendered it **increasingly ineffective**. Organizations can no longer rely on the assumption that **everything inside their network is secure**—instead, they must implement **identity-based access controls, continuous threat detection, and cloud-native security models** to protect their data and users.

As businesses continue to modernize their IT environments, the move away from perimeter-based security is **not just a trend—it's a necessity**. Adopting **Zero Trust, SASE, and AI-driven security frameworks** will ensure that organizations stay **resilient against evolving cyber threats** while enabling secure and scalable digital transformation.

Increasing Attack Surfaces with Cloud Adoption and Remote Work

The rapid adoption of **cloud computing and remote work** has fundamentally reshaped the way businesses operate, offering **unprecedented flexibility, scalability, and efficiency**. However, this digital transformation has also led to a significant expansion of **attack surfaces**, making organizations more vulnerable to cyber threats. Traditional security models, which relied on **well-defined network perimeters**, are struggling to keep up as critical data, applications, and workloads are now distributed across **cloud environments, SaaS applications, and remote endpoints**.

How Cloud Adoption Expands Attack Surfaces

The migration to cloud environments has introduced several **new security risks** that organizations must address. Unlike traditional on-premises infrastructure, where security teams had full control over firewalls, network segmentation, and access policies, **cloud services operate in shared, multi-tenant environments** managed by third-party providers. This shift brings several challenges:

1. **Loss of Direct Control:** In a cloud environment, businesses **rely on cloud service providers (CSPs)** for security, but they are still responsible for securing their own applications, configurations, and data (known as the **shared responsibility model**). Misconfigurations or weak access controls can lead to **data breaches, unauthorized access, and compliance violations**.
2. **Increased Complexity of Security Policies:** Organizations often use **multi-cloud and hybrid cloud architectures**, integrating services from AWS, Microsoft Azure, and Google Cloud. Each platform has different **security controls, logging mechanisms, and identity management policies**, making it difficult to enforce **consistent security standards** across environments.
3. **Cloud Misconfigurations:** One of the leading causes of cloud breaches is **misconfigured storage buckets, databases, and access controls**. Attackers actively scan the internet for exposed resources and **leverage automation to exploit misconfigured cloud assets**, leading to **data leaks and unauthorized access**.
4. **API and SaaS Security Risks:** Modern cloud applications rely heavily on **APIs (Application Programming Interfaces)** for communication. If APIs are improperly secured or exposed to the public, they can become an entry point for attackers to access **sensitive data or manipulate cloud services**.
5. **Lateral Movement in the Cloud:** Once attackers **gain a foothold in a cloud environment**, they can move laterally between workloads, escalate privileges, and compromise additional resources. Unlike traditional on-premise security, where segmentation was physical, **cloud environments require advanced micro-segmentation and identity-based access controls** to limit movement within the network.

The Security Challenges of Remote Work

As businesses embrace **remote work and hybrid work models**, they face **unprecedented security challenges** that stem from employees accessing corporate resources from **unsecured personal devices, home networks, and public Wi-Fi connections**. Some key security risks associated with remote work include:

1. **Unsecured Endpoints:** Many employees use **personal laptops, tablets, and smartphones** to access corporate applications. These devices may lack **endpoint security software, regular patching, and encryption**, making them easy targets for malware, ransomware, and phishing attacks.
2. **Increased Phishing and Social Engineering Attacks:** Cybercriminals have **exploited the rise of remote work** by launching sophisticated phishing campaigns. Attackers impersonate **IT support teams, cloud service providers, or company executives** to trick employees into revealing login credentials or downloading malicious files.
3. **VPN and Remote Access Vulnerabilities:** Many organizations rely on **VPNs (Virtual Private Networks)** to provide remote workers with secure access to internal resources. However, VPNs can be compromised through **stolen credentials, outdated software vulnerabilities, or misconfigured settings**. Additionally, once an attacker gains access through a VPN, they can often **move freely inside the corporate network**.
4. **Home and Public Network Risks:** Employees working from home often connect through **consumer-grade routers with weak security settings**, making their networks susceptible to **Wi-Fi hijacking, DNS spoofing, and man-in-the-middle**

(MITM) attacks. Similarly, working from **public Wi-Fi hotspots** (such as coffee shops or airports) exposes devices to **session hijacking and packet sniffing**.

5. **Lack of Centralized Security Controls:** Unlike traditional office environments, where IT teams could enforce **firewalls, access controls, and network monitoring**, remote work environments **lack direct oversight**. Organizations need to implement **cloud-based security solutions, endpoint protection, and Zero Trust frameworks** to ensure security across all remote endpoints.

The Role of Zero Trust and SASE in Addressing These Challenges

Given the **growing attack surface introduced by cloud adoption and remote work**, organizations must shift away from **perimeter-based security models** and adopt modern security frameworks like **Zero Trust and Secure Access Service Edge (SASE)**. These models provide:

1. **Zero Trust Access Controls:** Unlike traditional security models that assume trust for internal users, **Zero Trust enforces strict authentication and authorization** for every access request, regardless of location or device.
2. **Identity-Based Security:** Multi-Factor Authentication (MFA), **role-based access control (RBAC), and continuous identity verification** prevent unauthorized access.
3. **Cloud-Native Security Solutions:** SASE integrates **network security functions (firewalls, Secure Web Gateways, CASB, and Zero Trust Network Access) with cloud-based identity management**, ensuring **secure access to cloud applications and remote devices**.
4. **Endpoint and Threat Detection:** Organizations should deploy **advanced endpoint detection and response (EDR), security information and event management (SIEM), and real-time behavioral analytics** to monitor remote endpoints for suspicious activity.

Conclusion: The Urgent Need for Modern Security Strategies

As cloud adoption and remote work continue to rise, **attack surfaces will only expand**, creating **more opportunities for cybercriminals** to exploit vulnerabilities. Traditional security models that rely on **perimeter defenses and implicit trust** are no longer sufficient. Organizations must **embrace Zero Trust principles, deploy cloud-native security solutions, and invest in AI-driven threat detection** to **protect their data, users, and infrastructure in an increasingly digital world**.

By adopting **modern security frameworks like SASE, Zero Trust, and identity-based access controls**, businesses can **minimize risk, improve visibility, and strengthen their defenses** against evolving cyber threats. The future of cybersecurity depends on **adapting to the realities of a decentralized workforce and a cloud-first IT landscape**, ensuring that security is **built into every layer of the digital enterprise**.

Complex and Costly Infrastructure Maintenance

As businesses grow and their IT needs expand, maintaining traditional network and security infrastructure becomes increasingly **complex, resource-intensive, and expensive**. Legacy systems, including **on-premise firewalls, VPNs, intrusion detection systems (IDS), and data center hardware**, require **constant monitoring, patching, and upgrades** to remain effective against evolving cyber threats. These traditional architectures often lead to **operational inefficiencies, high capital expenditures (CapEx), and a growing burden on IT teams**, making it difficult for organizations to scale securely.

Challenges of Maintaining Traditional Network Infrastructure

1. **High Capital and Operational Costs**
   Maintaining a **traditional IT infrastructure** demands a **significant financial investment** in both hardware and software. Organizations must purchase **firewalls, switches, routers, load balancers, and security appliances**, which require periodic **upgrades and replacements**. Additionally, businesses incur **ongoing operational costs (OpEx)** for **software licensing, maintenance contracts, and vendor support**.

2. **Complexity in Managing Multiple Security Appliances**
   Legacy security architectures often rely on **multiple standalone appliances** for **firewall protection, intrusion prevention, secure web gateways, and VPN access**. Each of these systems requires **separate configuration, monitoring, and policy enforcement**, leading to **management overhead**. IT teams must ensure that security policies remain **consistent across all devices**, a task that becomes increasingly difficult in hybrid or multi-cloud environments.

3. **Frequent Software Patches and Firmware Updates**
   Network security devices and firewalls must be **regularly updated** with the latest **firmware patches and security definitions** to mitigate vulnerabilities. However, managing updates across **hundreds or thousands of devices** can be **time-consuming and prone to human error**, leaving gaps in security posture. Additionally, **downtime during updates** can disrupt business operations.

4. **Skill Gaps and IT Staff Burden**
   Managing **complex network infrastructure** requires a highly skilled IT workforce proficient in **network engineering, cybersecurity, and cloud integration**. As threats evolve, security teams must **constantly monitor logs, analyze threats, and fine-tune security policies**. The demand for **cybersecurity professionals far exceeds supply**, making it **challenging for organizations to hire and retain skilled personnel**. This skill gap increases reliance on **third-party managed services**, adding additional costs.

5. **Scalability Challenges with Traditional Architectures**
   Legacy security models were designed for **static, centralized networks**, where users and applications resided within **corporate data centers**. However, modern enterprises operate in **highly dynamic environments**, requiring rapid deployment of **new cloud services, remote access solutions, and IoT integrations**. Scaling traditional security infrastructure to accommodate this growth **requires substantial investment in new hardware, network redesigns, and additional security appliances**.

6. **Inconsistent Security Policies Across Multi-Cloud and Hybrid Environments**
   Businesses are increasingly adopting **multi-cloud and hybrid cloud architectures**, where applications and data are distributed across **public clouds (AWS, Azure, Google Cloud), private data centers, and SaaS platforms**. Managing **security policies across these diverse environments** can be extremely challenging, leading to **misconfigurations, policy mismatches, and security gaps** that attackers can exploit.

The Hidden Costs of Traditional Infrastructure Maintenance

Beyond the **direct costs** of hardware and software, businesses must also account for **hidden costs** associated with maintaining a traditional IT infrastructure:

- **Downtime and Productivity Losses**: Legacy systems often require **manual intervention** for troubleshooting, patching, and configuration changes, leading to potential **network outages** that impact business operations.
- **Compliance and Audit Expenses**: Industries with **strict regulatory requirements** (e.g., healthcare, finance, government) must ensure **continuous compliance** with standards such as **GDPR, HIPAA, and PCI-DSS**. Traditional security architectures require **manual auditing and compliance reporting**, which can be time-consuming and expensive.
- **Increased Risk of Cyberattacks**: As legacy systems age, they become **more vulnerable** to modern cyber threats. Maintaining older infrastructure often means **running outdated software**, which attackers exploit to **breach networks, steal data, or deploy ransomware**.
- **Energy and Space Costs**: On-premise data centers require **physical space, power, and cooling**, contributing to **high operational expenses**. Migrating to cloud-based security solutions can **eliminate these costs** and improve efficiency.

The Shift Towards Cloud-Based, AI-Driven Security Solutions

As maintaining traditional security infrastructure becomes **increasingly unsustainable**, organizations are shifting toward **cloud-native security solutions** that offer **scalability, automation, and cost savings**. The adoption of **Secure Access Service Edge (SASE)** and **Zero Trust architectures** is transforming how businesses secure their networks.

1. **Reduced Hardware and Maintenance Costs**
   Cloud-based security solutions eliminate the need for **on-premise security appliances**, reducing **hardware costs, upgrade expenses, and maintenance overhead**. Instead of managing **physical firewalls and VPN concentrators**, businesses can deploy **cloud-based firewalls, identity-driven access controls, and AI-powered threat detection**.
2. **Centralized Security Management**
   Instead of configuring multiple security appliances, organizations can **unify their security policies under a single cloud-based dashboard**. This simplifies **policy enforcement, monitoring, and compliance management**, reducing operational complexity.
3. **Automated Threat Detection and Response**
   AI-driven security platforms use **machine learning algorithms** to **detect and respond to cyber threats in real-time**. These solutions can **analyze network traffic, identify anomalies, and automatically block malicious activity**, reducing the burden on IT teams.
4. **Elastic Scalability**
   Unlike traditional infrastructure, which requires **manual hardware upgrades**, cloud-based security solutions can **scale dynamically** to accommodate business growth. Whether onboarding new remote workers, expanding cloud services, or integrating IoT

devices, security policies **adapt automatically** without requiring additional infrastructure investments.

5. **Enhanced Compliance and Visibility**
Cloud-native security solutions offer **built-in compliance monitoring, automated reporting, and continuous security assessments**, helping organizations meet **regulatory requirements with less manual effort**.

Conclusion: The Future of Network Security is Cloud-Driven

The complexity and cost of maintaining traditional security infrastructure **continue to rise**, making it **infeasible for modern enterprises** to rely on outdated network models. The shift to **cloud-native security, AI-driven automation, and Zero Trust principles** provides businesses with **scalability, agility, and improved threat protection** without the high operational burden.

By **adopting Secure Access Service Edge (SASE), Zero Trust Network Access (ZTNA), and AI-powered security analytics**, organizations can **streamline security management, reduce infrastructure costs, and future-proof their cybersecurity strategy** in an increasingly digital world.

Lack of Scalability and Flexibility for Modern Workloads

Traditional network security architectures were built for an era when IT infrastructure was centralized, applications were hosted on-premises, and most users worked from corporate offices. However, in today's digital-first world, enterprises operate across **distributed environments**, leveraging **cloud computing, SaaS applications, remote workforces, and hybrid IT models**. These modern workloads require **agile, scalable, and flexible security solutions**, which traditional security architectures often fail to provide.

Rigid Network Architectures Struggle to Scale

One of the fundamental limitations of **legacy security models** is their dependence on **static, perimeter-based defenses**, such as **firewalls, VPNs, and intrusion prevention systems (IPS)**. These solutions were designed for networks with **fixed endpoints** and **predictable traffic patterns**, making them ill-equipped to handle **dynamic workloads, cloud adoption, and remote access demands**.

1. On-Premises Firewalls and Security Appliances Are Resource-Intensive

Traditional security solutions rely on **hardware-based appliances** deployed at **corporate data centers** or branch offices. As businesses grow, scaling security infrastructure requires **purchasing and deploying additional firewalls, VPN concentrators, and security gateways**, leading to **high capital expenditures (CapEx) and operational costs (OpEx)**. Furthermore, provisioning and configuring new security appliances can take **weeks or months**, delaying business expansion and innovation.

2. Bottlenecks in Centralized Data Centers

Legacy security architectures typically route **all network traffic through a centralized data center** for inspection before granting access to cloud applications or external resources. This model creates **latency issues and network congestion**, especially when employees work remotely or access SaaS applications such as **Microsoft 365, Salesforce, or Google Workspace**.

For example, if a remote worker needs to access a cloud-based CRM tool, their traffic may need to be **backhauled through the corporate data center** for security checks before reaching its destination. This **reduces performance, increases bandwidth costs, and creates poor user experiences**.

3. VPNs and Traditional Remote Access Solutions Lack Flexibility

Virtual Private Networks (VPNs) were once the standard for **remote access security**, but they **lack scalability, performance, and granular access control**. As organizations shift to **remote work and hybrid environments**, VPN infrastructure **struggles to handle thousands of simultaneous connections**, leading to **performance degradation, security vulnerabilities, and management complexity**.

Additionally, VPNs operate on a **binary trust model**—once a user connects, they typically gain broad access to the corporate network, increasing the **risk of lateral movement** in the event of a security breach. This model is **incompatible with Zero Trust principles**, which require **least-privilege access and continuous verification**.

Modern Workloads Demand Scalability and Agility

To support **cloud-native applications, distributed workforces, and edge computing**, organizations require **security solutions that scale dynamically** without relying on hardware upgrades or manual configurations.

1. Cloud-First Environments Require Elastic Security

Modern businesses adopt **multi-cloud and hybrid cloud** architectures, where applications, data, and workloads are distributed across **AWS, Microsoft Azure, Google Cloud, and private data centers**. Traditional security solutions are not designed to **secure traffic across multiple cloud environments**, requiring organizations to implement **complex, fragmented security policies** across different platforms.

Cloud-native security solutions, such as **Secure Access Service Edge (SASE)**, provide **elastic security controls** that scale automatically as workloads expand, ensuring **consistent protection across on-prem, cloud, and remote environments**.

2. Edge Computing and IoT Introduce New Security Challenges

The rise of **edge computing** and **Internet of Things (IoT)** devices further highlights the limitations of traditional security. Organizations deploy **smart devices, industrial sensors,** and edge servers across **factories, remote offices, and mobile networks**, making it **impractical to rely on centralized security appliances**.

Security solutions need to **adapt to dynamic workloads**, enforcing **real-time security policies at the edge** without requiring traffic to be routed through a centralized data center. **Software-defined security architectures**, including **Zero Trust Network Access (ZTNA) and SASE**, provide **distributed security enforcement** that **scales with business needs**.

3. AI-Driven Security Provides Adaptive Protection

As cyber threats become **more sophisticated and fast-evolving**, organizations need **automated, AI-driven security** that adapts in real time. Traditional security models rely on **manual rule configurations, static policies, and reactive threat detection**, which cannot keep up with **advanced persistent threats (APTs), ransomware, and insider attacks**.

Cloud-based security solutions leverage **machine learning (ML) and artificial intelligence (AI)** to **analyze network traffic, detect anomalies, and automatically respond to threats**. This **automated scalability** allows businesses to **secure workloads without increasing IT complexity**.

The Shift to a Scalable and Flexible Security Model

To overcome the limitations of traditional security architectures, enterprises are increasingly adopting **cloud-native, identity-driven security models** that provide **scalability, agility, and automation**.

1. **Adopting Secure Access Service Edge (SASE)**
   a. SASE integrates **network security (firewall-as-a-service, secure web gateways, cloud access security brokers)** with **wide-area networking (SD-WAN)**, providing **scalable security across users, devices, and cloud environments**.
   b. Security is **delivered as a service**, reducing the need for **hardware appliances and manual maintenance**.
2. **Implementing Zero Trust Network Access (ZTNA)**
   a. Unlike VPNs, **ZTNA ensures that users and devices are continuously authenticated**, providing **granular, least-privilege access** to specific applications and resources.
   b. This model **eliminates lateral movement risks**, making it ideal for **remote work and cloud-based applications**.
3. **Leveraging AI-Driven Security Automation**
   a. AI-powered security platforms **automate threat detection, response, and policy enforcement**, reducing the burden on IT teams.
   b. Businesses can **scale security dynamically** without requiring **manual intervention or infrastructure upgrades**.
4. **Embracing Cloud-Native Security Platforms**
   a. Cloud-based security solutions **reduce dependency on on-premises hardware**, ensuring that security controls scale **seamlessly with business growth**.
   b. Organizations benefit from **centralized security policy management, real-time analytics, and automated compliance reporting**.

Conclusion: Future-Proofing Security for Scalability and Agility

In today's rapidly evolving digital landscape, organizations cannot afford to rely on **rigid, perimeter-based security models** that **fail to scale with modern workloads**. Traditional network security solutions **introduce bottlenecks, increase operational costs, and lack the flexibility needed to secure cloud-based applications, remote workers, and dynamic edge environments**.

By adopting **cloud-native security architectures, AI-driven automation, and Zero Trust principles**, businesses can achieve **scalable, flexible, and cost-effective security** that supports **modern IT environments**. The transition to **SASE, ZTNA, and software-defined security** is no longer a luxury—it is an **essential upgrade** for enterprises looking to **stay secure, competitive, and resilient in an era of digital transformation**.

Performance Issues Due to Backhauling Traffic Through Data Centers

As organizations increasingly adopt **cloud applications, SaaS platforms, and remote work**, traditional network architectures that rely on **backhauling traffic through centralized data centers** are becoming a major bottleneck. This outdated approach, originally designed for an era when most applications and data were hosted **on-premises**, now creates **latency, bandwidth congestion, and degraded user experiences**.

In a **backhauling model**, all user traffic—whether from remote workers, branch offices, or cloud applications—is first routed through a corporate data center for **security inspection and policy enforcement** before reaching its final destination. While this approach made sense when security tools were centralized within the data center, it is increasingly **inefficient and unsustainable** in today's **cloud-first, remote work, and mobile-driven environments**.

Increased Latency and Poor User Experience

One of the biggest drawbacks of backhauling traffic is the **added latency** it introduces. In a world where **real-time collaboration, video conferencing, and cloud applications** are mission-critical, increased latency can **frustrate employees, reduce productivity, and harm business operations**.

For example, if a remote employee in **New York** wants to access a **cloud-based CRM (like Salesforce)**, but their company's data center is in **San Francisco**, their traffic must **first be sent to San Francisco for security checks before reaching Salesforce's servers**. This unnecessary detour significantly increases the **round-trip time**, resulting in **slow application performance, long loading times, and a poor user experience**.

- **Cloud Applications Become Sluggish** – SaaS applications such as **Microsoft 365, Google Workspace, and Zoom** require low latency to function properly. When traffic is backhauled, users may experience **delayed responses, video buffering, and dropped calls**.

- **Remote Work Becomes Frustrating** – Employees working from home or mobile locations need **direct, low-latency access** to business applications. Forcing all traffic through a centralized data center **defeats the purpose of remote work flexibility** and can lead to constant performance complaints.

This problem is **exacerbated in global enterprises**, where employees and branch offices are spread across **different regions**. The further the data center is from the user, the **worse the performance degradation**.

Increased Bandwidth Costs and Network Congestion

Backhauling traffic also **wastes valuable bandwidth**, leading to **higher operational costs and congestion** in the corporate network.

Traditionally, organizations have **leased expensive MPLS (Multiprotocol Label Switching) lines** to ensure **high-performance private network connections** between branch offices and the data center. However, with the **massive increase in cloud and internet-based traffic**, MPLS links are struggling to handle the load, and upgrading them is **costly and inefficient**.

- **Cloud Services Create High Traffic Loads** – Employees accessing cloud applications **consume significant bandwidth**, and when this traffic is unnecessarily routed through the corporate data center, it clogs the network and creates bottlenecks.
- **Security Inspection Overhead** – Many companies backhaul traffic to apply **security policies using firewalls, intrusion prevention systems (IPS), and other security appliances**. As traffic volumes grow, these appliances **become overwhelmed**, leading to **delays in traffic processing and further slowing down network speeds**.

Additionally, **branch offices** that rely on backhauling face even **greater bandwidth constraints**. Instead of being able to **access cloud services directly over local internet connections**, their traffic must first be **tunneled through the data center**, unnecessarily consuming **corporate bandwidth and slowing down overall operations**.

Scalability Issues with Modern Business Growth

Backhauling creates **serious scalability challenges**, especially for businesses that are **rapidly expanding** their workforce, branch locations, and cloud adoption.

- **Increased Remote Work** – The rise of **hybrid and remote work models** means that more employees need secure access to cloud resources **without relying on the corporate data center**. Traditional backhauling models **were never designed for this level of remote access demand**.
- **Global Expansion Requires Decentralized Access** – Organizations with **international teams** cannot afford to **route all traffic through a single headquarters**. Employees in **Europe, Asia, or South America** need **direct access to cloud services without relying on a U.S.-based data center**.

- **Growing SaaS and IaaS Adoption** – As companies migrate to **AWS, Microsoft Azure, and Google Cloud**, forcing all traffic through a centralized location **defeats the purpose of cloud agility**. Cloud services are designed to be **accessed from anywhere**, but backhauling limits that flexibility.

For businesses looking to scale, **removing reliance on centralized data centers** is critical for ensuring **agility, growth, and seamless network performance**.

How Secure Access Service Edge (SASE) Eliminates Backhauling Problems

To address these performance challenges, organizations are turning to **Secure Access Service Edge (SASE)**, a cloud-native security model that **eliminates the need for backhauling traffic**.

1. Direct-to-Cloud Security with Cloud-Based Inspection

Unlike traditional architectures, **SASE applies security policies at the edge**, meaning traffic does not need to be **routed through a corporate data center** for inspection. Instead, security functions such as **firewall-as-a-service (FWaaS), secure web gateways (SWG), cloud access security brokers (CASB), and Zero Trust Network Access (ZTNA)** are delivered **directly from the cloud**.

2. Reducing Latency with Localized Security Enforcement

SASE providers have **global points of presence (PoPs)** that allow **traffic to be inspected closer to the user**, rather than forcing it to travel across long distances. This enables **low-latency, high-performance network access** for remote workers and branch offices.

3. Intelligent Traffic Routing and SD-WAN Integration

SASE incorporates **software-defined WAN (SD-WAN)**, which dynamically routes traffic over **the most optimal path**, reducing **congestion and improving performance**. Instead of **forcing all traffic through MPLS links**, SD-WAN enables **direct, secure access to cloud applications via the internet**, significantly improving **network efficiency and cost savings**.

Conclusion: Why It's Time to Move Away from Backhauling

The backhauling model was designed for a time when **applications were hosted in private data centers**, but in today's **cloud-first, remote-friendly world, it has become a major bottleneck**. Organizations that continue to rely on **backhauling traffic through centralized data centers** face:

☑ **Increased latency and poor user experience**
☑ **High bandwidth costs and network congestion**
☑ **Scalability challenges that limit business growth**

By adopting **SASE, Zero Trust, and SD-WAN**, businesses can **eliminate the need for backhauling, reduce latency, and improve security without sacrificing performance**. These modern security architectures provide **direct-to-cloud access, localized security enforcement, and intelligent traffic routing**, ensuring that users can **work efficiently from anywhere, without network slowdowns**.

For enterprises looking to **future-proof their network security**, **migrating away from backhauling** is no longer just an option—it is an **urgent necessity** for maintaining **business agility, performance, and security in the digital era**. 🚀

Security Gaps in Managing Mobile and Hybrid Workforce

The rapid rise of **mobile and hybrid workforces** has created **significant security challenges** for organizations. Employees today work from **multiple locations**, including **home offices, coffee shops, co-working spaces, and even while traveling**. While this flexibility improves productivity and work-life balance, it **stretches traditional security measures beyond their limits**, leaving organizations vulnerable to cyber threats.

Unlike the **centralized, office-based workforce of the past**, today's employees access **corporate networks, cloud applications, and sensitive data from personal and company-owned devices across various networks**. This shift introduces **new attack surfaces**, making it **difficult for IT teams to maintain visibility, enforce security policies, and protect enterprise assets**. Without a robust security framework in place, cybercriminals can exploit these vulnerabilities to launch **data breaches, ransomware attacks, and credential theft campaigns**.

1. Lack of Perimeter-Based Security in Remote Work

Traditional security models were built on the **idea of a fixed perimeter**—firewalls, intrusion prevention systems (IPS), and network access controls were deployed in **corporate data centers** to protect on-premise users and resources. However, **mobile and hybrid workforces operate outside of this perimeter**, making these security measures **largely ineffective**.

- Employees working from home or public Wi-Fi networks are often exposed to **man-in-the-middle (MITM) attacks, rogue Wi-Fi access points, and insecure connections**.
- Without **corporate firewalls and network-based threat detection**, remote workers may unknowingly download malware or access **phishing sites** that compromise corporate credentials.
- Cybercriminals exploit these weaknesses to **intercept data transmissions, inject malicious payloads, or launch session hijacking attacks**.

With employees **no longer confined to corporate networks**, organizations need to shift toward a **zero-trust security model**, where trust is never assumed, and **every device, user, and connection is continuously verified before granting access**.

2. Increased Risk of Credential Theft and Identity-Based Attacks

One of the biggest security gaps in managing a mobile workforce is the **reliance on weak or reused passwords**. Many employees **use the same credentials** across multiple accounts, making them easy targets for **credential stuffing and brute-force attacks**.

- Phishing attacks aimed at **stealing login credentials** have increased dramatically, as cybercriminals use fake emails, messages, and websites to **trick employees into revealing passwords**.
- The use of **personal devices (BYOD)** without strong authentication policies further increases the risk of unauthorized access to corporate systems.
- **Session hijacking and MFA bypass attacks** enable hackers to gain persistent access to cloud applications, even if multi-factor authentication (MFA) is in place.

To combat this, organizations should adopt **passwordless authentication, biometric security, and continuous identity verification**. Solutions like **Zero Trust Network Access (ZTNA)** enforce **strict identity validation policies** to ensure that **only authorized users can access corporate resources**, regardless of their location.

3. Data Leakage and Shadow IT from Uncontrolled Devices

A major concern with a mobile workforce is the **uncontrolled use of personal devices, applications, and cloud storage services**. Employees often bypass IT-approved security protocols by:

- Using **unauthorized cloud applications** (e.g., Google Drive, Dropbox, WeTransfer) to store or share sensitive business data.
- Accessing **corporate files from personal laptops, smartphones, or tablets** that lack endpoint security controls.
- Syncing business emails to **personal email clients**, increasing the risk of **data exfiltration** if the personal account is compromised.

This phenomenon, known as **Shadow IT**, exposes organizations to **compliance violations, intellectual property theft, and regulatory fines**. Without proper **data loss prevention (DLP) policies and cloud access security broker (CASB) solutions**, IT teams have **little to no visibility** into where corporate data is being stored, shared, or accessed.

To mitigate this risk, organizations should:

☑ **Enforce device compliance policies**, ensuring that only secure and managed devices can access corporate systems.

☑ **Implement DLP solutions** that detect and block unauthorized data transfers.

☑ **Use CASB tools** to monitor and secure **cloud applications**, preventing employees from using **unapproved file-sharing services**.

4. Vulnerabilities in Endpoint Security and Lack of Patching

With employees working outside of the corporate network, **endpoint security becomes the first line of defense**. However, many remote workers use **outdated operating systems, unpatched applications, and insecure home networks**, making them **prime targets for cyberattacks**.

- **Unpatched vulnerabilities** in Windows, macOS, and third-party software **leave endpoints exposed to exploits**.
- **Malware and ransomware attacks** are often deployed through **unsecured personal devices**, which can infect the entire corporate network once the user reconnects to company resources.
- Remote workers may **disable security updates or antivirus software** due to personal preferences, increasing the risk of compromise.

Organizations must enforce **strict endpoint security policies**, including:

☑ **Automatic patch management and vulnerability scanning** for all devices accessing corporate data.

☑ **Endpoint Detection and Response (EDR)** solutions to monitor for **suspicious activities and advanced threats**.

☑ **Remote wipe and encryption policies** to protect corporate data in case a **device is lost or stolen**.

5. VPN Vulnerabilities and Network Access Risks

Many organizations still rely on **Virtual Private Networks (VPNs)** for remote access, but VPNs **were not designed for large-scale remote workforces**. They introduce **security vulnerabilities**, including:

- **Single points of failure** – If a VPN server is compromised, attackers can gain **full access** to internal resources.
- **Lack of granular access control** – VPNs provide **broad network access** rather than limiting users to only the applications they need.
- **Slow performance and congestion** – VPN backhauling routes all traffic through a **centralized data center**, creating **latency issues** and reducing productivity.

Instead of relying solely on VPNs, organizations should migrate to **Zero Trust Network Access (ZTNA)**, which provides **granular, least-privilege access** to applications **without exposing the entire corporate network**.

6. Insider Threats and Lack of Visibility into User Activities

While external threats are a major concern, **insider threats**—whether **malicious or unintentional**—pose an equally dangerous risk to mobile and hybrid workforces.

- Employees may **intentionally exfiltrate sensitive data** before leaving the company.
- Accidental misconfigurations or **misuse of privileged access** can expose critical systems to cyberattacks.
- Without **behavioral analytics and continuous monitoring**, IT teams have **no way of detecting anomalies** that indicate suspicious activities.

To strengthen **insider threat detection**, companies should:

☑ **Implement User and Entity Behavior Analytics (UEBA)** to identify unusual access patterns.

☑ **Use Privileged Access Management (PAM)** to restrict high-risk administrative privileges.

☑ **Conduct regular security awareness training** to educate employees on the risks of **phishing, data sharing, and social engineering attacks**.

Conclusion: Addressing Security Gaps in Mobile and Hybrid Workforces

Managing security for a **mobile and hybrid workforce** requires a fundamental shift away from **traditional perimeter-based defenses**. Organizations must move toward a **Zero Trust security model**, enforcing strict identity verification, securing endpoints, and implementing **cloud-native security solutions like SASE (Secure Access Service Edge)**.

By addressing key security gaps—such as **endpoint vulnerabilities, VPN weaknesses, shadow IT risks, and identity threats**—businesses can ensure that **remote employees remain productive while maintaining strong cybersecurity defenses**. The future of work is **decentralized, cloud-driven, and mobile-first**, and security strategies **must evolve accordingly** to protect enterprises from modern threats. 🚀

Definition of SASE and How It Differs from Traditional Models

What is SASE?

Secure Access Service Edge (SASE), pronounced "sassy," is a **cloud-native architecture** that converges **network security and wide area networking (WAN) capabilities** into a single, integrated service. Coined by **Gartner in 2019**, SASE is designed to provide **secure, flexible, and efficient network access** for today's distributed workforce and cloud-driven enterprises. Unlike traditional security models that rely on **centralized, perimeter-based protections**, SASE **delivers security at the edge**, closer to users and applications, regardless of their location.

SASE **integrates several key network and security functions**, including:

☑ **Software-Defined WAN (SD-WAN)** – Provides intelligent traffic routing and optimized network performance.

☑ **Zero Trust Network Access (ZTNA)** – Ensures least-privilege, identity-based access to applications.

☑ **Cloud Secure Web Gateway (SWG)** – Protects against web-based threats such as malware and phishing.

☑ **Cloud Access Security Broker (CASB)** – Monitors and secures access to cloud applications.

☑ **Firewall as a Service (FWaaS)** – Delivers cloud-based firewall protection.

☑ **Data Loss Prevention (DLP)** – Prevents unauthorized data sharing and leakage.

By combining **networking and security into a single cloud-delivered service**, SASE eliminates the need for **disjointed, appliance-based security stacks** that traditional models rely on.

How SASE Differs from Traditional Security Models

Traditional network security models were built for an era when enterprises had **centralized offices, on-premise data centers, and a clearly defined security perimeter**. However, with the rise of **remote work, SaaS applications, and multi-cloud environments**, these models **no longer provide adequate protection**.

Here's how SASE fundamentally **differs from traditional security models**:

1. Centralized vs. Distributed Security Model

◆ **Traditional Security:**

- Security tools like **firewalls, intrusion prevention systems (IPS), and VPNs** are deployed in **on-premises data centers**.
- Remote users must **backhaul traffic** through these central locations for security inspection, **adding latency** and degrading performance.
- Security is **tied to fixed locations**, making it difficult to protect mobile workers and cloud applications.

◆ **SASE:**

- Security is **decentralized and cloud-native**, ensuring that policies follow users **wherever they go**.
- Users connect securely through **the nearest edge location**, reducing latency while maintaining protection.
- Eliminates the need to **route traffic back through corporate data centers**, improving performance.

Key Benefit: SASE **secures users at the edge**, allowing them to access cloud applications directly **without bottlenecks**.

2. VPN vs. Zero Trust Network Access (ZTNA)

- **Traditional Security:**

  - **VPNs** provide remote access by creating an **encrypted tunnel** between the user and the corporate network.
  - However, once inside, **VPN users have broad access** to the entire network, increasing **insider threats** and **lateral movement** risks.
  - VPNs struggle with **scalability**—they weren't designed for a workforce where **most employees work remotely**.

- **SASE (ZTNA-based Security):**

  - **Zero Trust Network Access (ZTNA)** replaces VPNs by enforcing **identity-based, least-privilege access** to applications.
  - Users only get access to **specific apps they need**, not the entire corporate network.
  - Reduces the **attack surface**, as hackers can't move laterally even if credentials are stolen.

Key Benefit: SASE with **ZTNA replaces VPNs**, offering **stronger security, granular access control, and improved scalability**.

3. Appliance-Based vs. Cloud-Native Security

- **Traditional Security:**

  - Requires **physical hardware (firewalls, IPS, SWG, and DLP appliances)** deployed in corporate offices.
  - Expensive to purchase, maintain, and scale, especially for **global enterprises**.
  - Updates and security patches must be managed **manually**, leading to security gaps.

- **SASE:**

  - Entire security stack is delivered **as a cloud service**—no need for physical appliances.
  - **Auto-updated in real time**, ensuring the latest threat protection **without manual patching**.
  - Easily scales **up or down** based on business needs, making it ideal for **growing enterprises**.

Key Benefit: SASE **eliminates hardware dependencies**, reducing costs and complexity while improving **agility and scalability**.

4. Network Performance and Traffic Optimization

- **Traditional Security:**

- All remote user traffic is **backhauled** to a central data center for security inspection.
- This adds **latency**, negatively impacting performance for SaaS applications like **Microsoft 365, Salesforce, and Zoom**.
- Doesn't optimize traffic routing, leading to **slow and inefficient connectivity**.

♦ **SASE (with SD-WAN):**

- Uses **Software-Defined WAN (SD-WAN)** to route traffic **dynamically based on performance needs**.
- Directs cloud traffic to the **nearest edge location**, improving speed and **user experience**.
- **Reduces congestion** and **latency issues** by eliminating unnecessary data center backhauling.

Key Benefit: SASE **optimizes application performance**, delivering faster, more reliable access to cloud services.

5. Static Perimeter vs. Identity-Driven Security

♦ **Traditional Security:**

- Security is based on **network location**—if you're inside the corporate network, you're trusted.
- This **perimeter-based approach** fails in modern environments where users work **from anywhere**.
- Attackers who bypass perimeter defenses gain **unrestricted access to internal systems**.

♦ **SASE:**

- Implements **Zero Trust principles**—every access request is **authenticated and verified** based on **identity, device, and risk level**.
- Security policies **follow users and devices**, ensuring protection **no matter where they connect from**.
- Reduces the risk of **internal threats, credential theft, and lateral movement attacks**.

Key Benefit: SASE **removes implicit trust** and enforces **strong security controls based on user identity and risk posture**.

Conclusion: Why SASE is the Future of Network Security

SASE represents a **paradigm shift** from traditional network security models that rely on **perimeter-based defenses and appliance-heavy architectures**. As organizations continue to embrace **cloud computing, hybrid work, and remote access**, legacy security approaches **fail to provide adequate protection** against modern cyber threats.

By converging **networking and security into a single cloud-delivered service**, SASE offers:

🚀 **Stronger security** with Zero Trust principles.

⚡ **Improved performance** with SD-WAN and edge-based enforcement.

📈 **Scalability and flexibility** to support modern workloads.

💰 **Lower costs** by eliminating expensive on-prem security appliances.

As cyber threats evolve and businesses become more decentralized, SASE **is no longer optional—it's essential** for enterprises looking to stay **secure, agile, and future-ready**.

Key Principles Behind SASE: Converging Networking and Security in the Cloud

The **Secure Access Service Edge (SASE)** model represents a fundamental shift in how enterprises approach **networking and security**. Instead of relying on **fragmented, on-premises security tools and network hardware**, SASE **integrates networking and security services into a unified, cloud-delivered framework**. This convergence **enhances security, improves performance, and enables scalability** for modern enterprises operating in an increasingly cloud-centric world.

Below are the **key principles that define the SASE framework** and explain why it is the **future of secure network architecture**.

1. Cloud-Native Architecture

Traditional networking and security solutions are heavily dependent on **physical hardware appliances**, such as **firewalls, VPN concentrators, and intrusion prevention systems (IPS)**. These systems require **constant maintenance, manual upgrades, and complex configurations**, making them inefficient in today's **dynamic cloud environments**.

SASE, on the other hand, is designed to be **cloud-native**. Instead of relying on **on-premise security appliances**, it delivers **security and networking functions as cloud services**. This means:

- **No need for physical hardware**—SASE is fully software-defined and managed in the cloud.
- **Automatic updates and threat intelligence**—Security patches, policies, and threat databases are updated in real-time without manual intervention.
- **Scalability**—Enterprises can **expand or shrink their security and networking capabilities** on demand, without purchasing additional hardware.

By leveraging the cloud, SASE eliminates **the bottlenecks and limitations of legacy security models**, ensuring that enterprises can **secure their networks efficiently and cost-effectively**.

2. Convergence of Networking and Security

One of the most defining aspects of SASE is its ability to **unify networking and security** into a single, seamless service. Traditionally, organizations have deployed **separate solutions for networking and security**, leading to **operational silos, complexity, and inefficiencies**.

For example, an enterprise may use:

- **SD-WAN for traffic routing,**
- **VPNs for remote access,**
- **Firewalls for perimeter security,**
- **Secure Web Gateways (SWG) for internet protection,**
- **Cloud Access Security Brokers (CASB) for SaaS security,**
- **Zero Trust Network Access (ZTNA) for identity-based access control.**

With SASE, **all these functions are integrated into a single cloud-delivered platform**, eliminating **incompatibility issues** and **reducing complexity**. This convergence enables:

- **Faster security enforcement**—Traffic does not need to be routed through multiple separate security devices.
- **Unified policy management**—Organizations can define and enforce security policies **centrally across all locations, devices, and users**.
- **Consistent security across all access points**—SASE ensures that security policies **follow users and devices**, regardless of whether they are on-premise, remote, or accessing cloud applications.

This **holistic integration** ensures that organizations can manage their networks **efficiently, securely, and with fewer operational overheads**.

3. Zero Trust Network Access (ZTNA) – Identity-Driven Security

A core principle of SASE is **Zero Trust Network Access (ZTNA)**, which **eliminates implicit trust** and enforces strict identity-based security controls. In traditional security models, users inside the corporate network are **automatically trusted**. This **perimeter-based approach** is no longer viable in an era of **remote work, cloud services, and mobile access**.

ZTNA follows the philosophy of **"Never Trust, Always Verify"**, meaning:

- **Users and devices must be authenticated before accessing any application or resource**.
- **Access is granted on a need-to-know basis**, reducing the risk of lateral movement by attackers.
- **Security is enforced at the edge**, ensuring that remote workers and cloud-based applications are protected **without relying on outdated VPN solutions**.

By integrating **ZTNA into SASE**, organizations can secure their networks **based on identity, device posture, and contextual risk factors**—rather than physical location.

4. Edge-Based Security Enforcement for Performance Optimization

One of the biggest challenges in traditional security models is **performance degradation** caused by **backhauling traffic** through corporate data centers for security inspection. This process:

- **Increases latency**—Data must travel long distances before reaching cloud applications.
- **Creates bottlenecks**—Centralized security appliances often struggle to handle increasing traffic loads.
- **Reduces user experience**—Employees experience slow connections when accessing SaaS applications.

SASE **solves this issue by enforcing security at the network edge**. Instead of routing traffic to a distant data center, SASE ensures that:

- **Security policies are applied at the nearest cloud point-of-presence (PoP)**, reducing latency.
- **Users can directly connect to SaaS applications and the internet securely**, without unnecessary delays.
- **Network performance is optimized using SD-WAN**, which dynamically selects the best network path based on **real-time conditions**.

This **edge-based security enforcement** ensures that enterprises **maintain high-speed connectivity without compromising security**.

5. Global Scalability and Simplified Management

Traditional security architectures are **rigid, complex, and difficult to scale**. Expanding a legacy network often requires:

- Purchasing additional **firewall appliances** and **VPN concentrators**.
- Manually configuring **new security rules and policies**.
- Managing security policies **across multiple locations and devices**.

SASE offers **global scalability and simplified management** by:

- **Delivering security as a cloud service**, which can be deployed instantly **across multiple locations**.
- **Providing a unified security dashboard**, where IT teams can manage security policies **centrally**.
- **Enabling flexible access control** for remote workers, branch offices, and cloud-based applications **without requiring physical infrastructure**.

By **eliminating on-premise security bottlenecks**, SASE enables organizations to scale **quickly, efficiently, and cost-effectively**.

6. Continuous Threat Intelligence and Adaptive Security

Cyber threats are evolving at an unprecedented pace, making it essential for organizations to adopt **proactive security strategies**. Traditional security models **struggle to keep up**, as they rely on **manual updates and reactive defenses**.

SASE incorporates **continuous threat intelligence** and **AI-driven security analytics** to:

- Detect and block **malware, phishing attacks, and ransomware** in real time.
- Adapt security policies dynamically based on **emerging threats and user behavior patterns**.
- Provide **automated responses** to mitigate security risks **before they cause damage**.

By leveraging **AI and real-time threat intelligence**, SASE ensures that security defenses remain **up-to-date and capable of stopping the latest cyber threats**.

Conclusion: Why SASE's Converged Model is the Future

The **traditional security model**—which relies on **disconnected point solutions, perimeter-based defenses, and centralized security stacks**—is no longer sufficient for modern enterprises. As organizations continue to embrace **cloud computing, remote work, and hybrid environments**, the need for a **scalable, flexible, and efficient security framework** has never been greater.

SASE provides a **cloud-native, identity-driven, and globally scalable approach** that:
- ☑ **Eliminates legacy security bottlenecks** by delivering security at the network edge.
- ☑ **Unifies networking and security** into a single, easy-to-manage platform.
- ☑ **Enhances performance** by reducing traffic backhauling and optimizing network paths.
- ☑ **Improves security posture** by enforcing Zero Trust policies and leveraging AI-driven threat intelligence.

By **converging networking and security in the cloud**, SASE enables enterprises to **adapt to evolving cyber threats, improve user experience, and reduce IT complexity**—making it a critical investment for organizations looking to secure their digital transformation. 🖋

Evolution of SASE as a Response to Modern Security Challenges

The rise of **cloud computing, remote work, mobile devices, and hybrid IT environments** has fundamentally changed the way businesses operate. While these advancements have improved **productivity and efficiency**, they have also **exposed critical security vulnerabilities** in traditional network architectures. The **Secure Access Service Edge (SASE)** framework emerged as a **direct response** to these modern security challenges, offering a cloud-native approach that integrates **networking and security** into a unified solution.

Understanding the **evolution of SASE** requires examining how legacy security models **failed to keep up** with the changing digital landscape and how SASE provides a **more scalable, flexible, and secure alternative**.

1. The Shift Away from Perimeter-Based Security

Historically, network security was built around the **castle-and-moat model**, where corporate data and applications were housed in **on-premise data centers**. Security measures like **firewalls, intrusion prevention systems (IPS), and Virtual Private Networks (VPNs)** were deployed at the **network perimeter** to control and filter access.

However, as businesses embraced **cloud services (SaaS, PaaS, IaaS), mobile workforces, and remote access**, this perimeter-based model became **obsolete**. Employees, partners, and third-party vendors began accessing corporate resources **from anywhere, on any device, over public networks**. This shift resulted in:

- **Increased attack surfaces**—Data was no longer confined to internal networks but distributed across multiple cloud platforms.
- **Complex security management**—Each cloud service required its own security controls, leading to **inconsistent policies and visibility gaps**.
- **Performance bottlenecks**—Routing traffic through centralized data centers for security inspection caused **latency and degraded user experience**.

Traditional security solutions simply **could not scale** to address these new realities, leading to the development of a **more dynamic and cloud-friendly approach—SASE**.

2. The Rise of Cloud Computing and SaaS Applications

One of the biggest drivers behind SASE's evolution was the **mass adoption of cloud-based applications**. Platforms like **Microsoft 365, Google Workspace, AWS, and Salesforce** became essential to business operations, replacing traditional on-premise software.

However, **legacy network architectures were not designed for cloud-first environments**. Many enterprises still relied on **Multiprotocol Label Switching (MPLS) networks and VPNs**, forcing remote users to connect back to a **corporate data center** before accessing cloud applications. This resulted in:

- **Poor application performance** due to unnecessary traffic backhauling.
- **Increased operational costs** from maintaining MPLS networks and VPN infrastructures.
- **Security blind spots**, as traditional firewalls could not inspect traffic flowing directly to cloud applications.

SASE **eliminates these inefficiencies** by delivering **networking and security services directly from the cloud**. Instead of backhauling traffic through a centralized location, SASE ensures that users connect to the nearest **cloud-based point-of-presence (PoP)**, improving performance while maintaining **consistent security policies across all locations**.

3. The Explosion of Remote and Hybrid Workforces

Another major challenge that led to SASE's rise was the **rapid expansion of remote work**. While remote access solutions like **VPNs** were once sufficient for occasional work-from-home scenarios, they quickly became **overwhelmed** when businesses had to support **hundreds or thousands of remote employees**.

Traditional **VPN-based security architectures failed** for several reasons:

- **Scalability issues**—VPN concentrators had limited capacity, leading to connection failures and bottlenecks.
- **Weak security**—VPNs provide broad network access once connected, making them **a prime target for cyberattacks**.
- **Inconsistent enforcement**—Remote employees often accessed corporate applications from **personal devices and unsecured networks**, creating gaps in security controls.

SASE addresses these issues through **Zero Trust Network Access (ZTNA)**, a fundamental component of its architecture. ZTNA ensures that **access to applications is granted on a least-privilege basis**, meaning users are **only allowed access to the specific resources they need**—without exposing the entire network. This shift from **network-centric** to **identity-based security** makes SASE a **superior alternative to VPNs** for securing remote and hybrid workforces.

4. Growing Cybersecurity Threats and Advanced Attacks

As cyber threats become **more sophisticated**, traditional security models have struggled to keep up. **Ransomware, phishing, supply chain attacks, and zero-day exploits** have all increased in frequency, and attackers have found ways to **bypass perimeter defenses** by targeting cloud applications and remote workers.

Legacy security models rely on **static security rules and appliance-based defenses**, which:

- **Require frequent manual updates**, creating gaps in protection.
- **Lack advanced threat intelligence**, making them ineffective against emerging threats.
- **Are difficult to scale**, leading to inconsistent security enforcement across different locations.

SASE **evolves security to be proactive** rather than reactive by incorporating **real-time threat intelligence, AI-driven analytics, and cloud-based security updates**. Security functions like **Secure Web Gateway (SWG), Cloud Access Security Broker (CASB), and Data Loss Prevention (DLP)** are delivered as **cloud services**, ensuring that enterprises receive **continuous security updates and automated threat detection** without relying on manual intervention.

5. The Transition from Hardware-Driven to Software-Defined Networks

In traditional IT environments, networking was heavily dependent on **physical hardware**, such as routers, switches, and firewalls. Scaling security and connectivity required **purchasing additional appliances**, configuring policies manually, and deploying them at multiple locations.

This approach was **time-consuming, costly, and rigid**, making it difficult for businesses to **adapt to changing demands**.

With the advent of **Software-Defined Networking (SDN) and Software-Defined Wide Area Networking (SD-WAN)**, enterprises gained **greater agility and flexibility**. SD-WAN enabled businesses to:

- **Optimize network traffic dynamically** based on real-time performance metrics.
- **Reduce dependency on MPLS networks** by utilizing broadband and direct-to-cloud connections.
- **Improve security integration** by enabling direct connectivity to **cloud security services**.

SASE takes **SD-WAN a step further** by **fully integrating security into the network fabric**, ensuring that every data packet is **inspected, encrypted, and secured at the network edge**. This **software-driven approach** allows businesses to scale **seamlessly** while maintaining **robust security protections**.

Conclusion: Why SASE is the Future of Network Security

The **evolution of SASE** is a direct response to the **limitations of traditional security architectures**. As enterprises increasingly rely on **cloud applications, remote workforces, and distributed networks**, they need a **security model that is agile, scalable, and built for the modern digital landscape**.

SASE provides this solution by:
☑ **Eliminating legacy perimeter-based security** and replacing it with **cloud-native, identity-driven security enforcement**.
☑ **Enhancing performance** by ensuring that security processing happens at the **network edge** rather than backhauling traffic.
☑ **Integrating Zero Trust principles** to secure remote workers, mobile users, and cloud-based applications.

☑ **Leveraging AI and real-time threat intelligence** to combat sophisticated cyber threats.

☑ **Simplifying IT operations** by consolidating multiple security and networking services into a **single, cloud-delivered platform**.

As businesses continue to **modernize their IT environments**, the adoption of SASE will become **essential** for maintaining **strong security, optimizing network performance, and enabling seamless digital transformation**.

Software-Defined WAN (SD-WAN) – Efficiently Managing Global Connectivity

As businesses expand their operations across multiple regions and embrace cloud-based applications, the need for **efficient, secure, and cost-effective wide-area networking (WAN) solutions** has never been greater. Traditional WAN architectures, which rely heavily on **Multiprotocol Label Switching (MPLS) and private circuits**, have struggled to keep pace with the demands of **global connectivity, cloud integration, and remote work**.

Software-Defined Wide Area Networking (SD-WAN) has emerged as a modern solution that **optimizes connectivity, enhances security, and improves network performance** while reducing costs. By leveraging **software-driven intelligence**, SD-WAN enables enterprises to manage their WAN infrastructure dynamically, ensuring **seamless, high-performance communication** across dispersed locations.

1. Challenges with Traditional WAN Architectures

Legacy WAN infrastructures were originally designed for an era where most applications and data resided within **on-premise data centers**. They relied on **MPLS circuits** to provide **secure and predictable connectivity**, but these architectures **were not built for the cloud era**.

Some major challenges enterprises face with traditional WAN models include:

- **High Costs** – MPLS circuits are expensive, especially for businesses that require global connectivity with **redundant and resilient network paths**.
- **Complex Configuration and Management** – Managing multiple network devices across multiple locations requires **manual configurations and extensive IT involvement**, leading to **higher operational costs**.
- **Limited Cloud Integration** – Traditional WAN architectures force **backhauling of traffic through central data centers**, which adds **latency and bottlenecks**, impacting the performance of cloud applications.
- **Lack of Application Awareness** – Legacy WAN solutions treat all traffic equally, failing to **prioritize mission-critical applications** like video conferencing, VoIP, and SaaS platforms.

SD-WAN was developed to address these issues by **decoupling network management from hardware-based infrastructure**, allowing businesses to create **more intelligent, flexible, and cost-efficient WAN environments**.

2. How SD-WAN Works: A Software-Driven Approach

SD-WAN introduces a **software-based abstraction layer** that **separates the control plane from the data plane**, enabling **centralized policy-based traffic management**. Instead of relying solely on **MPLS circuits**, SD-WAN enables enterprises to leverage multiple connection types, including:

- ☑ **Broadband Internet**
- ☑ **4G/5G LTE**
- ☑ **Fiber connections**
- ☑ **Satellite links**

By intelligently routing traffic across the **best available network paths**, SD-WAN ensures that applications receive **optimal performance and reliability** without depending on expensive private circuits.

The key components of SD-WAN include:

- **Centralized Orchestration** – SD-WAN uses a **cloud-based or on-premise controller** that allows IT teams to **define and enforce network policies globally** from a single dashboard.
- **Dynamic Path Selection** – Traffic is automatically routed over the most **efficient and cost-effective** network paths based on **real-time network conditions**.
- **Application-Aware Routing** – SD-WAN can prioritize latency-sensitive applications (e.g., **VoIP, video streaming, and CRM platforms**) while directing less critical traffic to lower-cost links.
- **Integrated Security** – Many SD-WAN solutions come with **built-in security features** such as **firewalling, encryption, intrusion prevention, and Zero Trust Network Access (ZTNA)**.

3. Benefits of SD-WAN for Global Connectivity

One of SD-WAN's biggest advantages is its ability to **connect global enterprise locations efficiently** while maintaining **high security and performance standards**. Some key benefits include:

🌐 *Enhanced Global Connectivity*

With SD-WAN, enterprises can **seamlessly connect branch offices, remote workers, and data centers worldwide** without relying solely on **expensive MPLS circuits**. It allows organizations to leverage **affordable broadband connections** while maintaining enterprise-grade performance.

💰 Cost Reduction and MPLS Optimization

By utilizing **multiple network connections**, SD-WAN significantly **reduces reliance on costly MPLS circuits**. Businesses can **blend MPLS, broadband, and LTE connections** to achieve **cost-efficient, high-performance WAN connectivity**.

🚀 Improved Application Performance

Unlike traditional WAN solutions, SD-WAN is **application-aware**—meaning it can **prioritize and optimize** mission-critical applications such as **Microsoft 365, Zoom, and Salesforce** while preventing congestion caused by less important traffic.

🔐 Integrated Security Features

SD-WAN solutions often incorporate **security capabilities** such as **end-to-end encryption, firewall policies, intrusion prevention, and Zero Trust Access**. By securing **traffic at the network edge**, SD-WAN helps prevent **cyber threats, data breaches, and unauthorized access**.

📈 Centralized Management and Automation

IT teams can manage **all network locations** from a **single cloud-based dashboard**, applying policies in **real-time** and reducing the need for **manual configuration at branch offices**. This improves **operational efficiency and network agility**.

⚡ Resilience and Redundancy

SD-WAN supports **automated failover mechanisms**—if one network connection experiences issues, traffic is instantly rerouted to a **more reliable connection**, ensuring **business continuity and minimal downtime**.

4. SD-WAN vs. Traditional WAN: A Side-by-Side Comparison

Feature	Traditional WAN	SD-WAN
Connectivity	MPLS-based, expensive	Hybrid (MPLS, broadband, LTE, fiber)
Performance	Static routing, congestion issues	Dynamic path selection, real-time optimization
Security	Perimeter-based, VPN-reliant	Integrated security with Zero Trust, encryption
Cloud Readiness	Backhauls traffic to data centers	Direct cloud access, optimized SaaS connectivity

Scalability	Complex, hardware-intensive	Software-driven, centrally managed
Cost	High MPLS costs, limited flexibility	Reduced costs, optimized bandwidth usage

5. SD-WAN and Secure Access Service Edge (SASE): A Perfect Match

While SD-WAN solves many **connectivity and performance issues**, it still **requires additional security** to protect against cyber threats. This is where **Secure Access Service Edge (SASE)** comes in—by **combining SD-WAN with cloud-delivered security services** such as:

- **Secure Web Gateway (SWG)**
- **Cloud Access Security Broker (CASB)**
- **Zero Trust Network Access (ZTNA)**
- **Firewall as a Service (FWaaS)**

SASE ensures that **network traffic is not only optimized for performance** but also **fully secured from cyber threats, data leaks, and unauthorized access**.

Together, **SD-WAN and SASE** provide a **comprehensive networking and security solution** that is:
- ☑ **Cloud-native**
- ☑ **Scalable**
- ☑ **Cost-efficient**
- ☑ **Optimized for remote work and digital transformation**

Conclusion: Why SD-WAN is Essential for Modern Enterprises

In today's digital world, enterprises need a **networking solution that is agile, scalable, and optimized for global connectivity**. **SD-WAN delivers on all fronts** by providing:

- **Seamless cloud integration** for SaaS and IaaS applications
- **Lower networking costs** with hybrid WAN connectivity
- **Enhanced security** through encrypted traffic and Zero Trust enforcement
- **Intelligent traffic management** for high-performance applications
- **Simplified operations** with centralized orchestration and automation

As businesses continue to expand their **cloud-first** and **remote work strategies**, **SD-WAN is no longer a luxury—it's a necessity**. When combined with **SASE**, organizations can achieve

the perfect balance of networking efficiency and robust cybersecurity, ensuring a **secure, high-performance global enterprise network**.

Zero Trust Network Access (ZTNA) – Eliminating Implicit Trust for Better Security

As cyber threats continue to evolve, traditional security models that rely on **implicit trust** are proving insufficient in protecting modern enterprises. **Zero Trust Network Access (ZTNA)** has emerged as a **foundational security framework** that eliminates implicit trust and enforces strict access controls based on identity, device posture, and security policies.

ZTNA is a **core component of the Zero Trust security model**, which operates on the principle of **"never trust, always verify."** Unlike traditional perimeter-based security, where users inside the corporate network are often trusted by default, ZTNA ensures that **all users, devices, and applications must be authenticated and authorized before gaining access to resources—regardless of their location**.

With the rapid adoption of **cloud applications, remote work, and hybrid IT environments**, ZTNA has become an essential approach for **enhancing security, reducing attack surfaces, and preventing lateral movement within networks**.

1. Why Traditional Access Models Are No Longer Sufficient

For years, enterprises relied on **Virtual Private Networks (VPNs) and perimeter-based security** to manage access to internal applications and data. The assumption was that once a user or device was authenticated, they could be **trusted** inside the network. However, this approach presents **major security risks** in today's dynamic IT landscape.

Some key challenges with traditional access models include:

* **Overly Broad Access** – VPNs grant users access to the entire internal network, increasing the risk of lateral movement in the event of a breach.
* **Lack of Granular Security Controls** – Once authenticated, users often have **persistent access** to resources, making it difficult to enforce dynamic policies.
* **Increased Attack Surfaces** – Remote workers, IoT devices, and cloud applications expand the attack surface, making traditional perimeter defenses ineffective.
* **Credential-Based Attacks** – Cybercriminals exploit stolen credentials through **phishing, brute-force attacks, and password reuse**, enabling unauthorized access.

ZTNA **addresses these security gaps** by shifting from a **network-centric** to a **user- and device-centric approach**, ensuring that access is granted **only when necessary, based on risk-based policies**.

2. How ZTNA Works: A Zero Trust Approach to Access Control

ZTNA fundamentally **removes the concept of implicit trust** and enforces a **least-privilege access** model. Instead of providing users with direct access to the network, ZTNA solutions act as an **intermediary**, verifying each access request **before granting permission**.

The **core principles** of ZTNA include:

✔ **Identity-Driven Access** – Users and devices must authenticate with **multi-factor authentication (MFA), single sign-on (SSO), and role-based policies** before accessing applications.

✔ **Context-Aware Verification** – Access is granted based on **device posture, location, behavior, and real-time risk assessments**.

✔ **Least Privilege Enforcement** – Users are only allowed **the minimum access needed** for their specific role and tasks.

✔ **Micro-Segmentation** – Instead of granting broad network access, ZTNA limits users to **specific applications and resources** they are authorized to use.

✔ **Continuous Monitoring** – Access is **not persistent**; users must be continuously **re-evaluated** based on risk levels and behavioral patterns.

ZTNA solutions typically operate in one of two ways:

1. **Endpoint-Initiated ZTNA** – A lightweight client agent is installed on the user's device to verify identity and posture before connecting to corporate resources.
2. **Service-Initiated ZTNA** – Applications are hidden from direct exposure to the internet, and access is only granted through a secure **broker** that mediates requests.

By implementing these approaches, **ZTNA reduces the attack surface, prevents unauthorized access, and significantly lowers the risk of lateral movement** within enterprise environments.

3. The Security Benefits of ZTNA

ZTNA provides **multiple security and operational advantages** that make it a **superior alternative** to legacy access control models like VPNs.

🔒 Stronger Protection Against Cyber Threats

ZTNA minimizes security risks by **removing implicit trust** and verifying every access attempt **in real-time**. This prevents **unauthorized users, compromised devices, and insider threats** from gaining access to sensitive resources.

⬡ Reduced Attack Surface

Unlike traditional networks that expose services to the internet, ZTNA **hides applications behind a secure access gateway**, making them invisible to attackers and preventing exploitation of open ports.

🗃 Improved Security for Remote and Hybrid Workforces

As employees work from **various locations and devices**, ZTNA ensures **secure access** without relying on a **VPN backhaul**, reducing latency while improving the user experience.

⬢ Preventing Lateral Movement in Breaches

If an attacker compromises a user's credentials, ZTNA prevents **lateral movement** by **limiting access to specific applications** instead of the entire network. This isolates potential threats and contains breaches before they spread.

❀ Adaptive, Context-Aware Security

ZTNA **dynamically adapts access permissions** based on user behavior, device health, and risk level. If suspicious activity is detected, access can be **immediately revoked** or **escalated for additional verification**.

💻 Simplified IT Management and Compliance

ZTNA enables IT teams to **centrally manage access policies, monitor security logs, and enforce compliance requirements** without the complexity of **managing VPN concentrators or perimeter firewalls**.

4. ZTNA vs. VPNs: Why ZTNA Is the Future of Secure Access

Feature	Traditional VPN	Zero Trust Network Access (ZTNA)
Access Model	Broad, network-wide access	Granular, least-privilege access
Trust Model	Implicit trust (after authentication)	Continuous verification (never trust, always verify)
Security Risks	Prone to credential theft, lateral movement	Restricts lateral movement, isolates threats
User Experience	VPN backhauling causes latency	Direct, optimized cloud and app access
Scalability	Limited, difficult to scale	Cloud-native, highly scalable

Device Security	No real-time posture assessment	Checks device posture and security status

Traditional VPNs were designed for **static, on-premises environments**—not for **cloud-first, remote workforces**. **ZTNA modernizes secure access**, providing **better security, performance, and scalability**.

5. ZTNA as a Core Component of Secure Access Service Edge (SASE)

ZTNA is a **fundamental building block of Secure Access Service Edge (SASE)**—a modern security framework that **combines networking and security in the cloud**.

SASE integrates ZTNA with **other cloud-delivered security services**, such as:

✔ **Secure Web Gateway (SWG)** – Protects users from web-based threats
✔ **Cloud Access Security Broker (CASB)** – Secures SaaS applications and data
✔ **Firewall as a Service (FWaaS)** – Provides cloud-based firewall protection
✔ **SD-WAN** – Enhances network performance and connectivity

By combining ZTNA with SASE, enterprises can achieve a **comprehensive security posture** that protects users, devices, and applications—regardless of their location.

Conclusion: Why Enterprises Should Adopt ZTNA Today

As organizations continue to embrace **cloud adoption, remote work, and hybrid IT environments**, traditional security approaches **can no longer keep up with modern threats. ZTNA provides a smarter, more secure way to grant access** by eliminating implicit trust and enforcing **real-time verification** for every connection.

- ◆ **Reduces attack surfaces and prevents unauthorized access**
- ◆ **Enhances security for remote and hybrid workforces**
- ◆ **Prevents lateral movement in the event of a breach**
- ◆ **Improves user experience without VPN bottlenecks**
- ◆ **Enables secure, scalable access for cloud-based applications**

By implementing ZTNA, enterprises can build a **future-proof security architecture** that **protects critical resources, reduces risk, and aligns with Zero Trust best practices**.

Cloud-Delivered Firewall as a Service (FWaaS) – Scalable and Distributed Firewall Protection

As enterprises increasingly migrate workloads to the cloud and adopt remote work models, **traditional on-premise firewalls are no longer sufficient** to secure modern, distributed networks. Enter **Firewall as a Service (FWaaS)**—a **cloud-delivered security solution** that provides **scalable, flexible, and globally distributed firewall protection** without the limitations of hardware-based security appliances.

FWaaS is a key component of the **Secure Access Service Edge (SASE)** architecture, offering **centralized policy enforcement, deep traffic inspection, and seamless protection for cloud and hybrid environments**. Unlike traditional firewalls that require physical deployment and maintenance, FWaaS **operates entirely in the cloud**, securing users, devices, and applications **regardless of their location**.

This shift from **hardware-centric security to a cloud-native model** enables enterprises to **reduce infrastructure complexity, enhance scalability, and improve security posture** in an era of increasing cyber threats and evolving digital transformation.

1. The Challenges with Traditional Firewall Architectures

For decades, organizations have relied on **on-premise firewalls** to secure their networks by inspecting and filtering traffic at the **perimeter**. However, the rapid adoption of **cloud services, remote workforces, and mobile devices** has significantly changed network security requirements.

Some of the key limitations of traditional firewalls include:

- **Perimeter-Based Security Model** – Traditional firewalls are deployed at data centers, enforcing security at the network's edge. However, as users and applications move to the cloud, this perimeter becomes increasingly irrelevant.
- **Lack of Scalability** – Expanding firewall capacity requires **purchasing and configuring new hardware**, which is costly and time-consuming.
- **Complexity of Policy Management** – Managing **multiple firewall appliances** across different locations results in **inconsistent security policies and operational overhead**.
- **performancee Bottlenecks** – As enterprises rely more on **cloud applications and SaaS platforms**, backhauling traffic through **on-premise firewalls** creates latency and degrades performance.
- **Limited Protection for Remote and Mobile Users** – Traditional firewalls struggle to secure remote workers who connect directly to cloud services **without passing through the corporate firewall**.

FWaaS **addresses these challenges** by moving firewall functionality to the **cloud**, where it can provide **consistent, scalable, and always-on protection** for users and applications—no matter where they are located.

2. What Is Firewall as a Service (FWaaS)?

Firewall as a Service (FWaaS) is a cloud-native security solution that delivers **firewall capabilities as a subscription-based service**, eliminating the need for physical firewall appliances. It provides **advanced security features, such as deep packet inspection (DPI), intrusion prevention (IPS), and zero-day threat protection**, all **without the constraints of hardware-based firewalls**.

With FWaaS, **all network traffic—whether from remote workers, branch offices, or cloud workloads—passes through a globally distributed cloud firewall infrastructure**, where **security policies are applied in real time**.

Key Features of FWaaS:

✔ **Cloud-Native Scalability** – Firewall protection **automatically scales** based on demand, without requiring hardware upgrades.

✔ **Centralized Security Policy Management** – Admins can define and enforce security rules **across all users, devices, and locations from a single control panel**.

✔ **Zero Trust Enforcement** – FWaaS integrates with **Zero Trust Network Access (ZTNA)** to ensure that users are verified before accessing resources.

✔ **Deep Packet Inspection (DPI)** – Examines **the entire packet payload** to detect threats, malware, and anomalies.

✔ **Secure Web Filtering** – Blocks **malicious websites, phishing attacks, and unauthorized content** based on predefined security policies.

✔ **Integration with SASE** – Works alongside **SD-WAN, ZTNA, CASB, and Secure Web Gateways (SWG)** for a **holistic cloud security approach**.

By moving firewall functions to **the cloud**, FWaaS ensures **consistent, robust security** for enterprises operating in a **decentralized, hybrid, or multi-cloud environment**.

3. How FWaaS Works: Cloud-Based Protection for Distributed Networks

Traditional firewalls **reside at the network perimeter**, inspecting incoming and outgoing traffic **within the corporate network**. FWaaS, on the other hand, **leverages cloud infrastructure to enforce security policies globally**, eliminating the need for backhauling traffic through on-premise firewalls.

Step-by-Step Process of FWaaS:

1 **Traffic is Routed to the FWaaS Cloud** – All enterprise traffic, whether from **remote users, branch offices, or cloud services**, is directed to the FWaaS platform for inspection.

2 **Identity and Context-Aware Security Policies Are Applied** – The firewall enforces **user-based and application-based access policies**, ensuring compliance with Zero Trust principles.

3 **Real-Time Threat Inspection and Filtering** – The system **analyzes network traffic, detects malware, blocks intrusions, and prevents data breaches** before traffic reaches its destination.

4 **Optimized Routing and Performance** – Unlike traditional firewalls that introduce latency, FWaaS integrates with **SD-WAN** to ensure optimized traffic flow and minimal disruptions.

5 **Continuous Monitoring and Adaptive Protection** – FWaaS continuously monitors **network behavior, user activity, and security threats**, adapting policies dynamically as risks evolve.

This **cloud-centric approach** enables enterprises to **simplify security management, enforce consistent policies, and protect remote and hybrid workforces seamlessly**.

4. Key Benefits of FWaaS

FWaaS provides **multiple advantages over traditional firewall solutions**, making it a **critical component of modern cybersecurity architectures**.

🌐 *Global, Scalable Security*

FWaaS operates **on a global cloud infrastructure**, ensuring **consistent protection** for users **regardless of their location**. Unlike hardware-based firewalls, which require **manual expansion**, FWaaS **scales dynamically** with business needs.

🚀 *Improved Performance and User Experience*

By eliminating the need to **backhaul traffic through centralized data centers**, FWaaS reduces **latency and bottlenecks**, ensuring a **faster, more efficient connection** to cloud applications.

🔒 *Stronger Security with Advanced Threat Protection*

FWaaS integrates **intrusion prevention, malware scanning, URL filtering, and DNS security** to provide **multi-layered protection against evolving cyber threats**.

📊 *Simplified Management and Cost Savings*

With FWaaS, enterprises no longer need to **purchase, configure, or maintain physical firewall appliances**. Security policies can be managed **from a single cloud-based dashboard**, reducing **operational complexity and IT overhead**.

FWaaS works in **tandem with other SASE components**, including **ZTNA, SD-WAN, Secure Web Gateways (SWG), and Cloud Access Security Brokers (CASB)**, ensuring **comprehensive, end-to-end security**.

5. FWaaS: A Critical Step Toward Modern Cybersecurity

As enterprises **embrace digital transformation, cloud-first strategies, and hybrid workforces**, legacy security solutions are proving **inefficient, costly, and difficult to manage**. FWaaS represents the **future of network security**, offering **scalable, flexible, and cloud-native firewall protection** that meets the demands of modern IT environments.

Organizations that adopt FWaaS can:

✔ **Strengthen security posture** with **real-time, globally distributed threat protection**

✔ **Reduce infrastructure complexity** by eliminating **hardware dependencies**

✔ **Improve performance and user experience** with **low-latency security enforcement**

✔ **Enable Zero Trust and SASE adoption**, ensuring **consistent security for all users and devices**

With the increasing sophistication of **cyber threats, cloud adoption, and remote work**, enterprises **must move beyond traditional firewalls** and embrace **cloud-delivered FWaaS to stay ahead of security challenges**.

Secure Web Gateway (SWG) – Filtering Web Traffic and Preventing Threats

As enterprises embrace cloud computing, remote work, and mobile access, ensuring **secure web access** has become a top priority. Traditional perimeter-based security solutions are no longer sufficient in an era where employees access cloud applications and corporate resources from **anywhere, on any device**. This shift necessitates a more **flexible, scalable, and intelligent** security approach—one that **filters web traffic, prevents threats, and enforces security policies** without impeding productivity.

This is where a **Secure Web Gateway (SWG)** comes in. SWG is a **cloud-based security solution** that protects users from **malware, phishing attacks, and unauthorized content** while enabling **secure access to web applications and cloud services**. It acts as a **protective barrier between users and the internet**, enforcing security policies in real-time to mitigate cyber threats before they reach corporate networks or endpoints.

With **cyber threats evolving rapidly**, organizations must **move beyond traditional firewalls and VPNs** and adopt **cloud-native security solutions** like SWG to ensure **safe, seamless, and policy-compliant** internet access for their workforce.

1. What Is a Secure Web Gateway (SWG)?

A **Secure Web Gateway (SWG)** is a **cloud-delivered or on-premise security solution** that **inspects, filters, and controls web traffic** to block **malicious websites, malware, data exfiltration, and unauthorized applications**. Unlike traditional firewalls, which focus on **network perimeter security**, SWG provides **real-time web security for users, regardless of location or device**.

SWG acts as an **intermediary** between users and the internet, enforcing security policies **before** users can access web content. It ensures that all web requests comply with **corporate security policies** while blocking **unsafe or non-compliant** traffic.

Key Functions of SWG:

✔ **URL Filtering** – Blocks access to **malicious, inappropriate, or non-work-related websites** based on predefined policies.

✔ **Threat Prevention** – Scans web traffic in real time to detect and block **malware, ransomware, and phishing attacks**.

✔ **Data Loss Prevention (DLP)** – Prevents **sensitive data from being leaked or stolen** via unauthorized web applications.

✔ **Content Inspection** – Deeply inspects encrypted and unencrypted web traffic for potential threats.

✔ **Cloud Application Control** – Monitors and manages access to cloud-based services such as **Google Drive, Dropbox, and Office 365**.

✔ **Inline Web Traffic Analysis** – Examines **real-time web traffic behavior** to identify suspicious patterns and block emerging threats.

Unlike **traditional firewalls or antivirus solutions**, which rely on **static rules and endpoint-based security**, SWG provides **dynamic, cloud-based protection** that scales with the needs of modern enterprises.

2. Why Traditional Web Security Is No Longer Enough

Legacy security models were built around **corporate networks**, where firewalls and intrusion detection systems protected users within a **defined perimeter**. However, the shift to **cloud computing, SaaS applications, and remote workforces** has rendered traditional web security approaches ineffective.

Challenges of Traditional Web Security:

◆ **Limited Visibility Over Web Traffic** – Legacy solutions lack **deep packet inspection capabilities**, making it difficult to analyze **encrypted web traffic** for threats.

◆ **Inadequate Protection for Remote Users** – Traditional firewalls and proxies require **traffic backhauling**, which increases latency and degrades user experience.

◆ **Rise of Shadow IT and Cloud Applications** – Employees frequently use **unsanctioned**

cloud services without IT approval, increasing the risk of data leaks and compliance violations.

 ◆ **Sophisticated Cyber Threats** – Attackers now use **advanced malware, phishing tactics, and zero-day exploits** that bypass legacy security measures.

By implementing an **SWG solution**, organizations can ensure **consistent security policies** for **all users, across all locations**, regardless of whether they are working **on-premises, remotely, or in the cloud**.

3. How a Secure Web Gateway Works

A **Secure Web Gateway** functions as a **filtering and inspection layer** between users and the internet. When a user attempts to access a website or cloud service, SWG evaluates the request **in real-time**, applying security policies before allowing or blocking the connection.

How SWG Processes Web Traffic:

1 **User Request** – A user attempts to access a website or web application (e.g., Office 365, YouTube, or a news website).

2 **Traffic Inspection** – SWG inspects **HTTP(S) requests** using deep packet inspection (DPI) to analyze **both metadata and content**.

3 **Threat Detection** – The system compares the request against **threat intelligence databases**, checking for **malware, phishing sites, or suspicious activity**.

4 **Policy Enforcement** – If the website is allowed, SWG ensures that **data protection and access policies** are followed. If the request violates security rules, the access is blocked.

5 **Logging and Reporting** – All traffic is logged for **auditing, compliance, and analytics**, helping IT teams identify and mitigate risks.

By performing **inline traffic analysis**, SWG prevents **malicious threats, unauthorized data transfers, and non-compliant web activity** before it can cause harm.

4. Benefits of Deploying a Secure Web Gateway (SWG)

The adoption of **SWG solutions** provides enterprises with **stronger web security, compliance enforcement, and performance optimization** in a cloud-first world.

🔒 **Stronger Cyber Threat Protection**

✔ Blocks **malware, ransomware, phishing, and zero-day attacks** before they reach users.
✔ Prevents **drive-by downloads** and malicious script execution from compromised websites.

📊 Improved Visibility and Compliance

✔ Provides **detailed logging and reporting** to ensure regulatory compliance (e.g., GDPR, HIPAA, SOC 2).

✔ Prevents **data exfiltration** by monitoring web-based file uploads and cloud interactions.

🚀 Optimized User Experience

✔ Eliminates the need to **backhaul internet traffic through data centers**, reducing latency and improving performance.

✔ Enables **fast, secure, and direct access to cloud applications** without compromising security.

🌐 Scalable, Cloud-Based Security

✔ Deploys security **as a cloud service**, eliminating the need for costly on-premises hardware.

✔ Scales dynamically to **support remote workforces and global enterprise networks**.

5. SWG as a Key Component of SASE

SWG is a **foundational element of Secure Access Service Edge (SASE)**, which **combines networking and security in the cloud**. In a SASE framework, SWG works alongside:

✔ **Zero Trust Network Access (ZTNA)** – Restricts access based on user identity and device posture.

✔ **Cloud Access Security Broker (CASB)** – Provides **visibility and control over cloud applications**.

✔ **Software-Defined WAN (SD-WAN)** – Enhances performance and security for remote and branch offices.

✔ **Firewall as a Service (FWaaS)** – Delivers **cloud-based firewall protection** for network traffic.

By integrating **SWG within a SASE architecture**, enterprises can **unify security policies, simplify management, and ensure secure access** for all users—**whether on-premises or remote**.

6. Conclusion: Why Enterprises Need SWG Today

The **modern workforce** is increasingly **mobile and cloud-driven**, making traditional network security models **obsolete. Secure Web Gateway (SWG)** is an **essential security**

solution that helps enterprises **filter web traffic, enforce policies, and block cyber threats** in real time.

By **adopting SWG**, organizations can:

✔ **Improve security posture** by blocking **web-based threats and malicious content**.

✔ **Enable remote work securely** without sacrificing performance.

✔ **Ensure compliance** with data protection and privacy regulations.

✔ **Reduce costs and complexity** by moving security to the **cloud**.

As cyber threats continue to evolve, enterprises must **transition from legacy security models to cloud-delivered solutions like SWG** to stay ahead of modern security challenges. 🚀

Cloud Access Security Broker (CASB) – Protecting Cloud Applications and Services

As enterprises increasingly migrate to **cloud-based applications and services**, the traditional security perimeter has all but disappeared. Employees now access corporate resources from **any location, on any device**, making it difficult for IT teams to monitor and secure data flow. The rise of **Software-as-a-Service (SaaS) applications, Infrastructure-as-a-Service (IaaS), and Platform-as-a-Service (PaaS)** has introduced new security challenges, including **data leakage, compliance violations, shadow IT, and account takeovers**.

To address these concerns, organizations need a **Cloud Access Security Broker (CASB)**—a **cloud-based security solution** that acts as an intermediary between **users and cloud applications**. CASB provides **visibility, compliance enforcement, data protection, and threat prevention** for cloud services, ensuring that businesses can adopt cloud technologies **without compromising security**.

1. What Is a Cloud Access Security Broker (CASB)?

A **Cloud Access Security Broker (CASB)** is a **security policy enforcement point** that sits **between cloud service users and cloud applications** to provide **visibility, security, and control** over cloud data and traffic. CASB enables organizations to enforce **security policies across all cloud services**, whether they are **sanctioned (approved by IT) or unsanctioned (shadow IT)**.

Unlike traditional security solutions that focus on **network perimeters**, CASB operates in the **cloud and applies security policies in real-time**, regardless of where users access their cloud services.

Key Functions of CASB:

✔ **Visibility & Shadow IT Discovery** – Identifies **all cloud services** used within an organization, even those not sanctioned by IT.

✔ **Data Protection** – Enforces **Data Loss Prevention (DLP) policies** to prevent **sensitive**

data leaks.

✔ **Threat Protection** – Detects and mitigates **malware, phishing attempts, and insider threats** in cloud environments.

✔ **Compliance & Policy Enforcement** – Ensures adherence to **regulations like GDPR, HIPAA, and SOC 2** for cloud data security.

✔ **Identity & Access Management** – Controls **who can access what data and applications** based on user identity, device, and location.

A **CASB solution** acts as a security checkpoint, applying **automated policies** to protect sensitive cloud data **before, during, and after** transmission.

2. Why Traditional Security Models Fail in the Cloud

Legacy security models were designed for **on-premises data centers**, where IT teams had **complete control** over applications, infrastructure, and security policies. However, with cloud adoption, **data moves beyond the corporate firewall**, making traditional security solutions **insufficient**.

Challenges of Traditional Security in a Cloud-First World:

◆ **Lack of Visibility into Cloud Usage** – Employees use cloud services **without IT approval**, leading to **shadow IT** risks.

◆ **No Granular Access Control** – Traditional **VPNs and firewalls** cannot enforce **identity-based security policies** for cloud applications.

◆ **Data Leakage Risks** – Cloud applications **store and share sensitive data**, but legacy solutions **lack control over data movement**.

◆ **Advanced Cyber Threats** – Hackers exploit **misconfigured cloud settings** and weak authentication to breach accounts.

◆ **Compliance Violations** – Many industries must comply with **data protection laws**, but organizations **struggle to monitor and enforce compliance in the cloud**.

A **CASB solution** addresses these challenges by providing **real-time security controls, deep visibility, and automated policy enforcement** for cloud environments.

3. How CASB Works to Secure Cloud Applications

CASB solutions **integrate seamlessly** with cloud applications via **APIs, proxies, or log analysis**, allowing organizations to **monitor, secure, and manage** cloud service usage in real time.

Four Pillars of CASB Functionality:

1 Visibility

- CASB discovers **all cloud applications** used within an organization, including **unsanctioned (shadow IT) apps**.
- Provides **detailed analytics** on **who is using what cloud service, from where, and on which device**.

2 Data Security

- Protects **sensitive data stored in the cloud** using **encryption, tokenization, and Data Loss Prevention (DLP) policies**.
- Prevents **unauthorized data sharing**, blocking accidental or intentional data exfiltration.

3 Threat Protection

- Detects and prevents **malware, ransomware, phishing attacks, and account takeovers**.
- Identifies **anomalous behavior**, such as **impossible travel scenarios** or **suspicious file downloads**.

4 Compliance

- Ensures adherence to **regulatory and industry-specific security requirements** (e.g., **GDPR, HIPAA, PCI-DSS**).
- Automates **policy enforcement** for cloud applications to maintain **audit readiness**.

CASB applies security controls at multiple levels—**before, during, and after data access**—ensuring **end-to-end cloud security**.

4. Key Benefits of CASB Adoption

Implementing a **CASB solution** provides organizations with **better control, visibility, and protection** over their cloud applications and data.

🔍 Comprehensive Visibility & Shadow IT Control

✔ Identifies **all cloud services** used across the organization.
✔ Helps IT teams understand **cloud usage trends and potential risks**.

🔒 Stronger Data Security & Compliance

✔ **Encrypts or tokenizes sensitive data** before storing it in the cloud.
✔ Prevents unauthorized **data sharing or downloads** using **DLP policies**.

🚀 Improved Threat Protection

✔ Detects **anomalous behavior, insider threats, and external attacks**.
✔ Prevents **malware, phishing, and ransomware infections in cloud environments**.

🌐 Secure & Seamless Cloud Access

✔ Enforces **granular access policies based on user identity, device, and location**.
✔ Reduces reliance on **VPNs and legacy perimeter security**.

By **integrating CASB into their security stack**, organizations can **securely adopt cloud technologies while maintaining full control over their data and compliance requirements**.

5. CASB as a Core Component of SASE

CASB is an essential part of Secure Access Service Edge (SASE)—a modern security framework that **converges networking and security into a cloud-based model**.

Within a **SASE architecture**, CASB works alongside:

✔ **Zero Trust Network Access (ZTNA)** – Enforces **identity-based access control**.
✔ **Secure Web Gateway (SWG)** – Protects users from **malicious websites and unsafe web traffic**.
✔ **Firewall as a Service (FWaaS)** – Delivers **cloud-based firewall protection**.
✔ **Software-Defined WAN (SD-WAN)** – Optimizes **secure cloud connectivity** for branch offices and remote users.

By integrating CASB with **SASE**, enterprises achieve **holistic security for cloud applications, networks, and users**, regardless of their location.

6. Conclusion: Why Organizations Need CASB Today

With the widespread adoption of **cloud computing, SaaS applications, and remote work**, organizations can no longer rely on **traditional security models** to protect their data. **Cloud Access Security Broker (CASB)** plays a crucial role in securing **cloud applications, preventing data breaches, and ensuring compliance**.

By deploying **CASB solutions**, enterprises can:

✔ **Gain deep visibility into cloud usage and shadow IT.**
✔ **Protect sensitive data through encryption and DLP.**

✔ **Enforce compliance with industry regulations.**

✔ **Detect and mitigate cloud-based threats.**

✔ **Enhance security within a SASE framework.**

As organizations continue their **digital transformation**, adopting **CASB** is no longer an option—it's a **necessity** to ensure **secure, scalable, and efficient cloud adoption.** 🚀

Data Loss Prevention (DLP) – Preventing Unauthorized Data Access and Leaks

Introduction to Data Loss Prevention (DLP)

As businesses continue to embrace **cloud computing, remote work, and digital collaboration**, the risk of **data breaches, leaks, and unauthorized access** has grown significantly. Organizations handle **sensitive data**, including **customer information, intellectual property, financial records, and confidential business strategies**, making it crucial to ensure **data security and compliance**.

Data Loss Prevention (DLP) is a **security strategy and set of tools** designed to **prevent unauthorized access, accidental sharing, or malicious exfiltration of sensitive data**. DLP solutions help organizations **monitor, classify, and control data movement across networks, endpoints, cloud services, and external devices** to ensure **compliance with security policies and regulatory requirements**.

1. Why is Data Loss Prevention (DLP) Essential?

Data is the **lifeblood of modern enterprises**, but it is also one of the **biggest security vulnerabilities**. Cybercriminals, insiders, and accidental misconfigurations can expose sensitive information, leading to **financial loss, legal consequences, and reputational damage**.

Key Drivers for DLP Implementation:

☑ **Prevent Data Breaches:** Cyberattacks, **phishing schemes, ransomware, and insider threats** can lead to **sensitive data exposure**. DLP protects against **unauthorized transfers**.

☑ **Ensure Regulatory Compliance:** Laws like **GDPR, HIPAA, PCI-DSS, and CCPA** impose strict **data protection mandates**. DLP helps businesses **enforce compliance policies and prevent fines**.

☑ **Protect Intellectual Property (IP):** Proprietary **business secrets, patents, research data, and product designs** can be targeted by **competitors or malicious insiders**. DLP ensures this data stays protected.

☑ **Control Insider Threats:** Employees may **accidentally or intentionally** leak sensitive data. DLP detects **unauthorized access attempts, email forwarding, or unapproved file transfers**.

☑ **Secure Cloud Collaboration:** As businesses rely on **Google Drive, Microsoft OneDrive, Dropbox, and other SaaS applications**, DLP ensures that sensitive files are not improperly shared or stored in unauthorized locations.

Without a **comprehensive DLP strategy**, organizations are at risk of **data exposure, compliance violations, and costly security incidents**.

2. How DLP Works: Key Mechanisms and Techniques

DLP solutions use a combination of **monitoring, analysis, classification, and enforcement techniques** to secure data. The technology operates across **endpoints, networks, and cloud environments** to identify and prevent data leaks.

🔍 Data Identification and Classification

DLP systems **scan, analyze, and categorize** data based on its **sensitivity, format, and content**. They use:

✔ **Pattern Matching:** Detects **Social Security Numbers (SSNs), credit card details, and other structured data** using predefined templates.

✔ **Fingerprinting:** Recognizes **specific confidential documents** based on unique signatures.

✔ **Metadata Analysis:** Classifies files based on **tags, keywords, or document properties**.

🚨 Policy-Based Access Control

DLP enforces **custom security policies** to control **who can access, share, or move sensitive data**. Policies can:

✔ **Block Unauthorized Transfers:** Prevent files from being emailed, uploaded, or copied to external drives.

✔ **Encrypt Data Automatically:** Ensure **sensitive data is encrypted before transmission**.

✔ **Redact Sensitive Information:** Hide or remove **sensitive details before a document is shared externally**.

📡 Network Traffic Monitoring

DLP solutions monitor **data-in-transit** across networks, flagging **suspicious email attachments, file transfers, or uploads**.

✔ Detects **unauthorized sharing of confidential documents** via email, FTP, or cloud storage.

✔ Monitors **unusual access attempts** from remote locations.

✔ Blocks **data exfiltration attempts by malware or rogue insiders**.

🖥️ Endpoint Protection

DLP tools secure **data on user devices**, preventing **USB data theft, screen capturing, and unauthorized printing**.

✔ Prevents **employees from copying sensitive files to personal USB drives or external devices**.

✔ Detects **screen-grabbing attempts by malicious software**.

✔ Blocks **unapproved file downloads from work computers**.

By combining **real-time monitoring, AI-driven analysis, and automated enforcement**, DLP solutions provide **robust security for enterprise data**.

3. Types of DLP Solutions

DLP strategies are deployed in **various environments** to protect data across **cloud, network, and endpoints**.

1 Network DLP (NDLP)

✔ **Monitors and secures data in transit** across corporate networks.

✔ Detects **unauthorized file transfers, email leaks, or data exfiltration attempts**.

✔ Prevents **accidental sharing of confidential information via email or cloud services**.

2 Endpoint DLP (EDLP)

✔ Secures data on **laptops, desktops, and mobile devices**.

✔ Blocks **file transfers to external drives, screenshots, or clipboard copying**.

✔ Detects **suspicious activity from insiders** who may be leaking data.

3 Cloud DLP (CDLP)

✔ Protects **data stored in cloud applications** like Google Drive, Office 365, and Dropbox.

✔ Prevents **sensitive information from being shared with unauthorized users**.

✔ Ensures **compliance with cloud security policies**.

Modern enterprises often **combine all three types** for **comprehensive data protection**.

4. Challenges of Implementing DLP

Despite its effectiveness, **DLP adoption comes with challenges** that organizations must address:

✏ **Complexity in Policy Management** – Defining and enforcing **DLP rules** for different departments and data types can be challenging.

✏ **False Positives and False Negatives** – Overly strict DLP policies **may disrupt legitimate work**, while lenient policies may **fail to detect real threats**.

✏ **User Resistance and Productivity Concerns** – Employees may find **DLP restrictions inconvenient**, leading to **workarounds or shadow IT**.

✏ **Cloud & BYOD Risks** – Protecting data on **personal devices (Bring Your Own Device - BYOD) and cloud platforms** requires **continuous monitoring**.

To address these challenges, organizations must **fine-tune DLP policies, educate employees, and integrate AI-driven automation**.

5. The Role of DLP in a Secure Access Service Edge (SASE) Model

As businesses transition to **Secure Access Service Edge (SASE)**, DLP becomes an essential component of **modern cloud security**.

✔ **Works with Zero Trust Network Access (ZTNA)** to ensure **data security at all access points**.

✔ **Enhances Secure Web Gateway (SWG)** by filtering **sensitive data from web traffic**.

✔ **Integrates with Cloud Access Security Broker (CASB)** to protect **cloud-stored data**.

By embedding **DLP within SASE**, organizations achieve **stronger data protection, regulatory compliance, and cloud security**.

6. Conclusion: Why DLP is Critical for Modern Enterprises

With cyber threats growing and data regulations tightening, **Data Loss Prevention (DLP) is no longer optional—it's a necessity**. Whether an organization handles **financial records, healthcare data, or trade secrets**, a **DLP solution safeguards business-critical information**.

By implementing **network, endpoint, and cloud-based DLP strategies**, businesses can:

✔ **Prevent unauthorized access and data exfiltration.**

✔ **Ensure compliance with GDPR, HIPAA, PCI-DSS, and more.**

✔ **Protect sensitive information from cyber threats and insider risks.**

✔ **Reduce financial losses and reputational damage from data breaches.**

In an era where **data security defines business success**, DLP solutions empower organizations to stay ahead of evolving threats and compliance challenges. 🚀

Zero Trust Model for Stronger Access Controls

Introduction to Zero Trust Security

As cyber threats become more **sophisticated and pervasive**, traditional security models that rely on **implicit trust** are no longer sufficient. The **Zero Trust model** has emerged as a **proactive and modern approach** to access control and cybersecurity, eliminating the outdated notion that users and devices inside the corporate network should be automatically trusted.

Zero Trust security operates under a simple principle: "Never trust, always verify." This means that every user, device, and application attempting to access corporate resources must be **continuously authenticated, authorized, and validated**, regardless of whether they are inside or outside the corporate network.

In an era where **remote work, cloud computing, and mobile access** have expanded the attack surface, organizations must adopt **Zero Trust strategies** to protect their assets from both **external cybercriminals and insider threats**.

1. Why Traditional Security Models Are No Longer Effective

Traditional security architectures were built on a **perimeter-based approach**, often compared to a castle-and-moat system. In this model:

☑ Firewalls and VPNs are used to create a **secure perimeter**.

☑ Users and devices **inside the network** are considered **trusted**.

☑ Once a user gains access, they often have **unrestricted movement** within the network.

This approach worked **reasonably well** in the past when corporate data and applications were hosted **on-premises**, and employees worked **within office buildings**. However, with the rise of:

- **Cloud-based applications and storage** (e.g., Google Workspace, Microsoft 365, AWS)
- **Remote and hybrid workforces** accessing company resources from personal devices
- **IoT and mobile devices** increasing network entry points

- **Sophisticated cyber threats** such as **phishing, ransomware, and supply chain attacks**

The traditional perimeter has **eroded**, making it easy for **attackers to bypass outdated security measures**. Once an attacker breaches the perimeter, they can move **laterally across the network**, accessing sensitive data without additional authentication.

This **lack of granular access control** has led to major security breaches, pushing organizations to adopt a **Zero Trust model**.

2. Core Principles of the Zero Trust Model

The **Zero Trust security framework**, developed by **Forrester Research** and promoted by organizations like **NIST and CISA**, is built on several fundamental principles:

🔍 1. Verify Every User and Device

Unlike traditional security models that assume users inside the network can be trusted, **Zero Trust requires continuous authentication**. This means:

✔️ **Multi-Factor Authentication (MFA):** Users must provide multiple forms of verification (e.g., password + biometric scan).
✔️ **Device Posture Assessment:** Checks if a device has the latest **security patches, antivirus software, and compliance settings**.
✔️ **Risk-Based Authentication:** Adjusts security policies based on user behavior, location, and login patterns.

🔄 2. Least Privilege Access (LPA)

Zero Trust enforces the **Principle of Least Privilege (PoLP)**, ensuring users and devices only have **the minimum access required** to perform their tasks. This minimizes **unauthorized access risks** and prevents attackers from escalating their privileges.

✔️ **Role-Based Access Control (RBAC):** Users only access **specific data and applications relevant to their job**.
✔️ **Just-In-Time (JIT) Access:** Access is granted **only when needed** and revoked automatically after use.
✔️ **Micro-Segmentation:** Divides the network into smaller segments to **limit lateral movement** if a breach occurs.

🌐 3. Assume Breach Mentality

Zero Trust operates under the assumption that:
✔️ **Threat actors are already inside the network** or could gain access at any moment.

✔ Security policies should focus on **detecting and mitigating threats in real time**.

✔ **Continuous monitoring** is necessary to track user behavior and flag suspicious activities.

🔑 4. Secure Access to Cloud and SaaS Applications

With businesses shifting to cloud environments, Zero Trust extends **beyond traditional data centers** to **cloud platforms, SaaS applications, and remote endpoints**.

✔ **Cloud Access Security Brokers (CASB):** Enforce policies for cloud applications.

✔ **Secure Web Gateways (SWG):** Monitor and filter internet traffic.

✔ **Identity and Access Management (IAM):** Controls authentication and permissions.

🛡️ 5. Implement Strong Endpoint Security

Endpoints, including laptops, mobile devices, and IoT systems, are common targets for cyber threats. **Zero Trust requires endpoint security solutions** to ensure these devices are:

✔ **Compliant with security policies** before accessing the network.

✔ **Protected by Endpoint Detection and Response (EDR)** solutions.

✔ **Monitored for anomalies and suspicious behavior** in real time.

3. Zero Trust Technologies and Implementation

To enforce **Zero Trust security**, organizations deploy a combination of technologies:

1 Identity and Access Management (IAM)

IAM solutions ensure **only authorized users and devices** can access enterprise resources.

- **Multi-Factor Authentication (MFA)**
- **Single Sign-On (SSO)**
- **Biometric Authentication**
- **Risk-Based Authentication**

2 Zero Trust Network Access (ZTNA)

ZTNA replaces **traditional VPNs** by enabling **secure, identity-based access** to specific applications rather than entire networks.

- **Prevents lateral movement by attackers**
- **Reduces attack surface by hiding internal applications from the public internet**
- **Enforces continuous verification of users and devices**

③ Micro-Segmentation

Micro-segmentation **breaks the network into smaller, isolated zones**, preventing attackers from **moving freely** if they gain access.

- **Restricts user access to only necessary systems**
- **Prevents malware from spreading across the network**
- **Enhances security for cloud and hybrid environments**

④ Endpoint Detection and Response (EDR) & Extended Detection and Response (XDR)

These solutions continuously **monitor, analyze, and respond** to endpoint security threats in real time.

- **Detects malware, ransomware, and insider threats**
- **Automates security responses based on AI-driven analytics**
- **Reduces dwell time of cyber threats**

⑤ Secure Access Service Edge (SASE)

SASE integrates **Zero Trust principles** with **cloud-based security** to protect **remote users, cloud applications, and corporate networks**.

- **Combines ZTNA, SWG, CASB, FWaaS, and DLP**
- **Delivers security at the network edge, reducing latency**
- **Ideal for modern, distributed enterprises**

4. Benefits of Zero Trust for Modern Enterprises

By implementing **Zero Trust security**, organizations gain:

✔ **Stronger Access Controls** – Ensures users, devices, and applications are continuously verified.

✔ **Reduced Attack Surface** – Limits opportunities for cybercriminals to exploit vulnerabilities.

✔ **Improved Compliance** – Meets data security regulations such as **GDPR, HIPAA, and PCI-DSS**.

✔ **Minimized Insider Threat Risks** – Prevents unauthorized data access and lateral movement.

✔ **Enhanced Cloud Security** – Protects workloads and applications in **multi-cloud environments**.

5. Conclusion: Zero Trust is the Future of Cybersecurity

In today's **hybrid workforce and cloud-first world**, the traditional **perimeter-based security model is obsolete**. The **Zero Trust approach** provides a **modern, adaptive security framework** that ensures **continuous verification, least privilege access, and proactive threat detection**.

By integrating **Zero Trust with Identity Management, ZTNA, Micro-Segmentation, and Endpoint Security**, businesses can effectively **protect their digital assets, reduce risks, and enhance resilience** against cyber threats.

With **Zero Trust**, organizations shift from a **reactive security approach to a proactive, intelligent defense strategy**—making it a **must-have for securing the modern enterprise**. 🚀

Continuous Security Enforcement Across Users, Devices, and Applications

Introduction: The Need for Continuous Security

In today's **digital-first, cloud-driven world**, organizations face an **ever-expanding attack surface**. Employees work from **multiple locations**, access **corporate data from various devices**, and use **a mix of on-premise, cloud, and SaaS applications**. This dynamic environment makes it **challenging to maintain security** using traditional, perimeter-based security models.

To combat these challenges, businesses are shifting towards **continuous security enforcement**—a **proactive approach** that ensures **ongoing protection, monitoring, and adaptation** to threats in real time. Unlike traditional security models that rely on **one-time authentication or static policies**, continuous security enforcement **dynamically assesses and enforces security policies** based on **user behavior, device posture, and application risk**.

1. Why One-Time Authentication and Static Security Policies Are Not Enough

Historically, security models were built on a **single authentication event**—a user logs in, gains access, and remains trusted throughout their session. However, this approach is **highly vulnerable** to modern cyber threats such as:

- **Stolen Credentials** – Attackers using phishing or credential stuffing can impersonate legitimate users.
- **Session Hijacking** – Malicious actors intercept authenticated sessions to gain unauthorized access.
- **Insider Threats** – Employees with valid credentials may **intentionally or accidentally** leak sensitive data.

- **Device Compromise** – A trusted device may become infected with **malware or ransomware** after authentication.

To address these risks, security enforcement must **go beyond initial authentication** and apply **continuous monitoring, risk assessment, and adaptive policy enforcement** throughout a session.

2. Key Pillars of Continuous Security Enforcement

🔍 1. Continuous Authentication and Identity Verification

Instead of verifying users only at login, continuous authentication dynamically re-evaluates their trust level throughout their session. This approach uses:

✓ **Behavioral Biometrics** – Analyzes typing patterns, mouse movements, and keystroke dynamics to detect anomalies.
✓ **Risk-Based Authentication** – Adjusts authentication requirements based on login location, device health, or unusual access patterns.
✓ **Adaptive Multi-Factor Authentication (MFA)** – Triggers additional authentication steps when a session shows suspicious activity.

If a user's behavior deviates from their normal pattern, security systems can **prompt for re-authentication or terminate access automatically**.

📟 2. Device Posture Assessment and Continuous Monitoring

In a world where employees use a **mix of corporate and personal devices**, ensuring **device security** is critical. Continuous security enforcement assesses:

✓ **Device Compliance Checks** – Ensures that devices have **up-to-date antivirus, security patches, and endpoint protection**.
✓ **Zero Trust Network Access (ZTNA)** – Restricts access based on device risk levels, preventing compromised devices from connecting to sensitive resources.
✓ **Endpoint Detection and Response (EDR/XDR)** – Monitors devices for **malware infections, unauthorized access attempts, or unusual activity**.

If a device falls out of compliance (e.g., an outdated OS or suspicious activity is detected), security policies can **automatically revoke access or quarantine the device**.

🌐 3. Real-Time Application and Data Security Enforcement

Applications and cloud services **store and process business-critical data**, making them prime targets for cyberattacks. **Continuous security enforcement applies protection mechanisms across all applications**, including:

✓ **Cloud Access Security Broker (CASB)** – Monitors and enforces security policies for SaaS and cloud applications, preventing unauthorized data sharing.

✓ **Secure Web Gateway (SWG)** – Inspects internet traffic to block access to **malicious websites, phishing links, and shadow IT applications**.

✓ **Data Loss Prevention (DLP)** – Continuously scans for **sensitive data movement** and blocks unauthorized file transfers or leaks.

By continuously monitoring application usage, organizations can detect and **stop security violations in real time**.

3. AI and Machine Learning in Continuous Security

To make continuous security enforcement **scalable and efficient**, organizations are leveraging **Artificial Intelligence (AI) and Machine Learning (ML)**. These technologies allow security teams to:

✓ **Analyze user and network behavior** to establish baselines and detect anomalies.

✓ **Automate response actions** to mitigate threats in real time.

✓ **Predict potential security breaches** before they happen, using historical attack patterns.

For example, if a user who typically logs in from **New York suddenly accesses the system from Russia**, AI-driven security can **trigger additional verification steps or block access** until further validation is completed.

4. Benefits of Continuous Security Enforcement

By implementing continuous security enforcement, organizations gain:

✓ **Stronger Protection Against Insider and External Threats** – Ensures **no implicit trust**, reducing the risk of credential theft and insider attacks.

✓ **Improved User Experience** – Instead of forcing **all users** through rigid security measures, continuous security adapts **dynamically based on risk levels**, making authentication seamless for legitimate users.

✓ **Real-Time Threat Detection and Response** – Security teams can **identify and neutralize threats immediately**, rather than reacting **after a breach occurs**.

✓ **Compliance and Regulatory Adherence** – Continuous monitoring helps organizations meet **GDPR, HIPAA, PCI-DSS, and SOC 2** security requirements.

5. Implementing Continuous Security in a Zero Trust Framework

Continuous security enforcement is a **core pillar** of the **Zero Trust model**, which assumes **all users, devices, and applications are potential security risks**.

To implement continuous security effectively, organizations should:

1️⃣ **Adopt Zero Trust Network Access (ZTNA)** to replace outdated VPNs and enforce **identity-based access controls**.

2️⃣ **Leverage AI-driven Security Analytics** to **monitor user behavior and detect anomalies** in real time.

3️⃣ **Integrate Endpoint Security Solutions (EDR/XDR)** to ensure all devices are **secure before granting access**.

4️⃣ **Use Adaptive Access Controls** that **continuously evaluate risk and enforce security dynamically**.

5️⃣ **Deploy a Cloud-Native Security Stack**, including CASB, SWG, and DLP, to **protect cloud applications and data**.

6. Conclusion: The Future of Cybersecurity is Continuous

As cyber threats evolve, organizations **can no longer rely on static, one-time security measures. Continuous security enforcement** is essential to **adapting to dynamic threats, reducing attack surfaces, and safeguarding critical assets** across **users, devices, and applications**.

By embracing **real-time monitoring, AI-driven analytics, and adaptive security policies**, businesses can build **a resilient, future-proof cybersecurity strategy** that **ensures security without compromising productivity**.

🔹 **The future of cybersecurity is continuous, intelligent, and Zero Trust-driven—making it the most effective defense against today's complex threat landscape.** 🚀

Better Security in a Cloud-First World

Introduction: The Shift to a Cloud-First World

Organizations worldwide are embracing a **cloud-first** strategy, prioritizing cloud computing for their applications, data storage, and IT infrastructure. Cloud services provide **scalability, flexibility, and cost efficiency**, enabling businesses to operate efficiently and innovate rapidly. However, this shift also introduces **new security challenges** that traditional on-premise security models were never designed to handle.

As cyber threats become more sophisticated and attack surfaces expand, organizations must **rethink their security approach**. Cloud security must be **holistic, continuous, and adaptive**, ensuring that **users, data, applications, and devices remain protected—regardless of location or network boundaries**.

1. The Limitations of Traditional Security in a Cloud-First Environment

Historically, **security was built around the corporate perimeter**—protecting an organization's internal network using **firewalls, VPNs, and intrusion prevention systems**. However, as businesses migrate to **cloud-based applications like Office 365, Google Workspace, AWS, and Azure**, traditional security models have **become ineffective** because:

✓ **Perimeter-Based Security is Obsolete** – Employees, customers, and partners access corporate resources from **anywhere, anytime**, making perimeter-based defenses inadequate.

✓ **VPNs Are Not Scalable** – Legacy VPNs cause **latency, bottlenecks, and security risks**, as they grant broad access to corporate resources.

✓ **Cloud Applications Increase Attack Surfaces** – Businesses rely on multiple SaaS applications, making it difficult to **monitor and control access**.

✓ **Data is No Longer Centralized** – With **hybrid and multi-cloud** environments, data is stored in different locations, increasing the risk of data exposure.

To address these challenges, organizations must adopt **cloud-native security frameworks** that protect assets **regardless of location or infrastructure**.

2. Key Security Challenges in a Cloud-First World

🌍 Expanding Attack Surfaces

With employees accessing corporate resources from **multiple locations and devices**, cybercriminals exploit vulnerabilities through:

✓ **Phishing and Credential Theft** – Cloud-based applications rely on passwords, making them prime targets for **phishing, brute-force attacks, and credential stuffing**.

✓ **Misconfigured Cloud Environments** – Cloud misconfigurations can expose **sensitive data to the internet**, leading to massive breaches.

✓ **Third-Party Risks** – Businesses integrate with **third-party vendors and APIs**, increasing the risk of supply chain attacks.

🔐 Weak Identity and Access Management (IAM)

Many cloud breaches occur due to **poor identity management practices**, such as:

✓ **Overly Permissive Access** – Employees often have more privileges than necessary, increasing **the risk of insider threats**.

✓ **Lack of Multi-Factor Authentication (MFA)** – Without MFA, stolen passwords **can be easily exploited** by attackers.

✓ **No Continuous Authentication** – Traditional IAM systems verify users **only at login**, leaving sessions vulnerable to **hijacking or credential theft**.

🗁 Data Security and Compliance Risks

✓ **Data Sprawl Across Multi-Cloud Environments** – Sensitive data is stored **across different cloud platforms**, making **visibility and control difficult**.

✓ **Regulatory Compliance Challenges** – GDPR, HIPAA, and SOC 2 require businesses to **enforce strict data protection measures**.

✓ **Data Loss and Unauthorized Sharing** – Without **Data Loss Prevention (DLP) policies**, sensitive data may be accidentally or intentionally **leaked via cloud applications**.

To combat these risks, **cloud-first security** must focus on **identity-driven access controls, real-time monitoring, and proactive threat prevention**.

3. The Role of Cloud-Native Security Architectures

A cloud-first world requires **cloud-native security solutions** that are designed to **protect users, applications, and data—regardless of network boundaries**. These solutions include:

🛡 Zero Trust Network Access (ZTNA) – Eliminating Implicit Trust

Zero Trust operates on the principle of **"never trust, always verify."** It enforces:

✓ **Least Privilege Access** – Users and devices are given **only the access they need**, reducing lateral movement.

✓ **Continuous Authentication** – Identity is verified **at every access request, not just at login**.

✓ **Microsegmentation** – Limits access between workloads to **minimize attack surfaces**.

ZTNA **replaces VPNs** by granting **secure, conditional access** to cloud applications without exposing the entire network.

🌐 Secure Access Service Edge (SASE) – Converging Network and Security

SASE combines **network security and cloud-based security services** into a unified model. It includes:

✓ **Software-Defined WAN (SD-WAN)** – Ensures **fast, secure, and optimized connectivity** across multiple cloud providers.

✓ **Cloud-Delivered Firewall as a Service (FWaaS)** – Provides **scalable firewall**

protection without traditional hardware limitations.

✓ **Cloud Access Security Broker (CASB)** – Monitors and controls access to **SaaS applications**.

✓ **Secure Web Gateway (SWG)** – Blocks **malicious web traffic, phishing attempts, and shadow IT usage**.

By adopting SASE, organizations gain **scalability, better performance, and stronger security—without relying on traditional data center backhauling**.

📊 AI-Driven Threat Detection and Response

Modern security solutions leverage **AI and machine learning** to:

✓ **Detect anomalies and behavioral patterns** in real time.

✓ **Automate response actions** to mitigate threats instantly.

✓ **Reduce false positives** by continuously refining security models.

AI-powered security enables **proactive defense** against **zero-day attacks, insider threats, and account takeovers**.

4. Strengthening Cloud Security with Best Practices

To achieve better security in a cloud-first world, organizations should follow these best practices:

✓ **Adopt a Zero Trust Security Model** – Implement **least privilege access and continuous authentication**.

✓ **Enforce Multi-Factor Authentication (MFA) Everywhere** – Protect all user logins, cloud apps, and privileged accounts.

✓ **Use Cloud-Native Security Solutions** – Deploy **SASE, ZTNA, CASB, and FWaaS** to secure all cloud resources.

✓ **Monitor and Audit Cloud Environments Continuously** – Use **AI-driven security analytics** to detect **suspicious activity**.

✓ **Implement Strong Data Protection Policies** – Use **Data Loss Prevention (DLP)** and **encryption** to protect sensitive data.

✓ **Secure API and Third-Party Integrations** – Regularly assess **supply chain risks and external connections**.

By implementing these strategies, businesses can **build a resilient cloud security posture** that adapts to evolving threats.

5. Conclusion: Security Must Evolve With the Cloud

As businesses continue to adopt **cloud-first strategies**, cybersecurity must evolve **beyond traditional defenses**. The shift to **Zero Trust, SASE, and AI-driven security** ensures that organizations remain **protected in an ever-changing digital landscape**.

Key Takeaways:

✓ **Traditional security models are no longer effective in a cloud-first world.**

✓ **Organizations must adopt Zero Trust principles, SASE frameworks, and AI-driven security analytics.**

✓ **Continuous monitoring, identity-based access controls, and proactive threat detection are essential.**

✓ **Security should be built into cloud strategies—not treated as an afterthought.**

By prioritizing **cloud-native security approaches**, businesses can ensure that **their digital transformation is not just efficient—but also secure.** 🚀

How SASE Enhances Performance and User Experience

Introduction: The Need for Speed and Security

As businesses transition to cloud-based applications, remote work, and digital-first operations, **network performance and user experience** become critical factors. Employees, customers, and partners expect **fast, seamless, and secure access** to applications—whether they are in the office, working remotely, or accessing services across the globe. However, **traditional network security models** often introduce latency, bottlenecks, and inefficiencies, leading to **frustrated users and reduced productivity**.

Secure Access Service Edge (**SASE**) solves these challenges by **integrating networking and security into a cloud-native architecture**. Unlike traditional models that **backhaul traffic through centralized data centers**, SASE dynamically routes traffic through **the most optimal paths**, ensuring **better performance, reduced latency, and enhanced security**.

1. Eliminating Data Center Bottlenecks

The Problem with Backhauling Traffic

Traditional network architectures are designed with **data centers as central hubs**. In this model, all user traffic—whether it originates from a remote office, a home network, or a mobile device—must first be routed through **on-premise firewalls, VPN concentrators, and security appliances** before reaching its destination. This approach, known as **backhauling**, results in:

✓ **High Latency** – Users experience delays as traffic takes an unnecessary detour to the corporate data center before reaching cloud applications.

✓ **Bandwidth Congestion** – Increased traffic leads to **slow application performance** and **video conferencing issues**.

✓ **Poor Remote User Experience** – Remote employees **suffer from slow connections** when accessing business-critical applications.

How SASE Fixes It

SASE **distributes security and network functions across globally dispersed cloud points of presence (PoPs)**. Instead of sending traffic to a central data center, users connect to **the nearest PoP**, where security policies are enforced **in real-time**. This results in:

✓ **Reduced Latency** – Traffic follows the shortest, most efficient path to cloud applications.

✓ **Optimized Performance** – Cloud-based security functions are processed closer to users.

✓ **Consistent User Experience** – Employees, partners, and customers enjoy **faster and more reliable access** to applications and data.

2. Optimizing Cloud Application Performance

The Challenge of Cloud Connectivity

With businesses adopting **SaaS applications like Microsoft 365, Google Workspace, and Salesforce**, network infrastructure must evolve. Traditional security solutions **struggle to efficiently handle direct-to-cloud traffic** due to:

✓ **Unoptimized Routing** – Legacy security architectures force traffic through inefficient paths.

✓ **VPN Bottlenecks** – Remote users accessing SaaS applications over VPN connections experience **slow performance and frequent disconnections**.

✓ **Lack of Application Visibility** – IT teams cannot monitor or control how applications behave across distributed networks.

SASE's Performance Benefits

By integrating **Software-Defined WAN (SD-WAN) with security services**, SASE enables:

✓ **Direct-to-Cloud Access** – Traffic is sent directly to SaaS applications through the nearest cloud PoP, reducing network congestion.

✓ **Intelligent Traffic Steering** – SASE dynamically routes traffic over the **best-performing network paths** using **real-time analytics**.

✓ **Application-Aware Prioritization** – Business-critical applications receive **higher priority** for bandwidth and performance optimization.

With SASE, employees can collaborate in **real-time** on cloud applications **without experiencing slowdowns or disconnections**.

3. Improving Remote Work and Hybrid Workforce Connectivity

Traditional VPNs vs. SASE

Remote workforces rely on **Virtual Private Networks (VPNs)** for secure connectivity. However, VPNs create **significant performance and security issues**, such as:

✓ **Overloaded VPN Gateways** – Too many remote users connecting to a single VPN concentrator **slows down network performance**.

✓ **Latency from Tunneling** – VPNs **encrypt and reroute** all traffic, even for public cloud applications, increasing **response times**.

✓ **Broad Network Access Risks** – VPNs grant users excessive network access, increasing **security vulnerabilities**.

How SASE Enhances Remote Work Performance

SASE replaces **traditional VPNs with Zero Trust Network Access (ZTNA)**, offering:

✓ **Secure, Direct Application Access** – Instead of tunneling traffic through a VPN, users securely connect to applications via **the nearest SASE PoP**.

✓ **Seamless Performance Optimization** – **AI-driven traffic optimization** ensures low latency and high availability.

✓ **Granular Access Controls** – Users only access **what they need**, reducing security risks while improving connection speeds.

By eliminating **VPN bottlenecks** and enforcing **intelligent routing**, SASE ensures **remote workers experience smooth and secure connectivity**.

4. Enhancing Security Without Slowing Down Performance

The Trade-Off Between Security and Speed

In traditional security models, organizations must **choose between performance and security**. Firewalls, proxies, and VPNs introduce **latency**, slowing down connections to cloud applications. This forces IT teams to **either weaken security policies or frustrate users with slow access speeds**.

SASE's Cloud-Native Security Benefits

SASE **solves the performance-security trade-off** by embedding security directly into the network, leveraging:

✓ **Cloud-Delivered Firewall as a Service (FWaaS)** – Instead of relying on hardware firewalls, security enforcement happens **at the cloud edge**, improving speed and scalability.

✓ **Secure Web Gateway (SWG) – Filters malicious traffic** without slowing down web access.

✓ **Cloud Access Security Broker (CASB)** – Provides **real-time visibility and control over SaaS applications** without impacting user experience.

✓ **Zero Trust Security Model – Verifies every connection dynamically**, eliminating unnecessary authentication delays.

With **security and networking integrated into the same framework**, SASE ensures **strong protection while maintaining high performance**.

5. AI-Driven Traffic Optimization and Intelligent Routing

The Role of AI in Network Performance

SASE leverages **artificial intelligence (AI) and machine learning (ML)** to analyze and optimize network traffic in real-time. AI-powered features include:

✓ **Dynamic Path Selection** – Traffic is **automatically routed** through the fastest and most reliable network paths.

✓ **Predictive Analytics** – AI identifies network congestion and **adjusts routing** before slowdowns occur.

✓ **Automated Threat Detection** – AI-powered security engines detect and mitigate threats **without human intervention**, reducing response times.

By using AI-driven analytics, **SASE ensures users experience faster, more reliable, and more secure network connections**.

Conclusion: Why SASE is Essential for Performance and User Experience

SASE **revolutionizes networking and security** by delivering **fast, secure, and optimized access** to applications, data, and services. Unlike traditional models that create **bottlenecks and latency issues**, SASE:

✓ **Eliminates Data Center Backhauling** – Users connect **directly to cloud applications** for **faster access speeds**.

✓ **Optimizes Cloud and SaaS Performance** – AI-driven traffic steering ensures **smooth collaboration** across cloud applications.

✓ **Enhances Remote Work Connectivity** – Zero Trust Network Access (ZTNA) **replaces** slow VPNs with **seamless, direct access**.

✓ **Delivers Security Without Performance Trade-Offs** – Integrated security functions **operate at the cloud edge**, eliminating slowdowns.

✓ **Uses AI for Continuous Optimization** – Network performance is dynamically adjusted **to provide the best possible experience**.

By **converging networking and security** into a **cloud-native, AI-driven model**, SASE ensures that organizations can operate **efficiently, securely, and without performance limitations**.

As businesses continue to **embrace remote work, cloud services, and digital transformation**, adopting SASE is no longer an option—it is a **necessity for superior performance and user experience**. 🚀

How SASE Simplifies Network and Security Management

Introduction: The Complexity of Traditional Network Security

Modern enterprises operate in a highly dynamic and distributed environment, where applications, data, and users are no longer confined to on-premise networks. Organizations now rely on **cloud services, remote workforces, mobile devices, and globally distributed offices**, all of which introduce **complex security and networking challenges**.

Traditional approaches to network security **require multiple disparate solutions**, such as **firewalls, VPNs, intrusion detection systems, cloud security gateways, and access control mechanisms**. Managing these fragmented tools leads to **operational inefficiencies, security gaps, and increased costs**.

Secure Access Service Edge (**SASE**) simplifies network and security management by **converging security and networking into a single, cloud-native architecture**. It streamlines operations, enhances security, and **provides centralized visibility and control**—all while reducing complexity and cost.

1. Converging Networking and Security into One Framework

The Problem: Too Many Disparate Security and Networking Tools

Traditionally, network security involves **multiple, separate solutions** deployed at different locations, including:

- Firewalls
- VPNs for remote access

- Secure Web Gateways (SWG)
- Cloud Access Security Brokers (CASB)
- Intrusion Prevention Systems (IPS)
- Data Loss Prevention (DLP)
- Software-Defined WAN (SD-WAN)

Each of these **tools operates independently**, requiring separate configurations, monitoring, and policy enforcement, leading to:

✓ **Operational Overhead** – IT teams must manage **multiple vendors, interfaces, and configurations**.

✓ **Inconsistent Security Policies** – Security rules vary across **on-premise, cloud, and remote environments**, creating vulnerabilities.

✓ **Visibility Challenges** – Lack of a **centralized management system** makes it hard to track network traffic and security events.

How SASE Fixes It

SASE **unifies networking and security functions** into a **single, cloud-delivered architecture**. Instead of deploying and maintaining **multiple appliances**, organizations can manage everything through a **centralized control plane**, which includes:

✓ **Integrated Security and Network Policies** – SASE enforces security and networking policies consistently across **all users, devices, and locations**.

✓ **Cloud-Native Deployment** – Security services (e.g., CASB, SWG, FWaaS, ZTNA) are delivered via **cloud points of presence (PoPs)**, reducing reliance on on-premise appliances.

✓ **Simplified IT Operations** – Instead of managing multiple vendors and configurations, IT teams can use **one unified platform**.

By replacing fragmented solutions with **a single, cohesive architecture**, SASE **reduces complexity and improves security enforcement**.

2. Centralized Policy Management and Visibility

The Challenge of Managing Security Policies Across Multiple Locations

In traditional networks, policies must be configured **separately** for different security appliances and locations. For example:

- **On-premise firewalls** have their own rules for filtering traffic.
- **Cloud security gateways** require separate configurations.
- **Remote access VPNs** enforce different access policies.
- **Data centers and branch offices** each have unique security settings.

Managing security policies across **these different environments** is complex, time-consuming, and **prone to misconfigurations**, increasing security risks.

How SASE Improves Policy Management

SASE provides a **centralized policy management system**, allowing IT teams to define security and networking rules **once and apply them everywhere**. Benefits include:

✓ **Unified Security Policies** – Organizations can enforce **the same security policies across all locations**, whether users are in the office, working remotely, or accessing cloud applications.

✓ **Real-Time Policy Updates** – Changes to security rules can be **instantly propagated** across the entire network.

✓ **Consistent Compliance Enforcement** – Compliance policies (e.g., GDPR, HIPAA, SOC 2) are **automatically applied** across all environments.

With SASE, IT teams no longer have to configure **multiple security appliances manually**. Instead, they **define policies once and enforce them across the entire network**.

3. Reducing Complexity with Cloud-Native Security

The Problem with Traditional Security Appliances

Legacy network security relies heavily on **physical hardware appliances** such as firewalls, VPN concentrators, and intrusion prevention systems. These on-premise devices create several challenges:

✓ **Hardware Maintenance** – IT teams must **install, update, and replace** hardware appliances, leading to **high operational costs**.

✓ **Scalability Issues** – Expanding security coverage **requires purchasing additional hardware**, which is expensive and time-consuming.

✓ **Manual Updates** – Security patches and threat updates must be **manually installed**, delaying protection against new cyber threats.

How SASE Uses Cloud-Native Security

SASE eliminates the need for **on-premise security appliances** by delivering security **as a cloud service**. Benefits include:

✓ **Scalable Security** – Organizations can **expand security coverage instantly** without purchasing additional hardware.

✓ **Automatic Updates** – SASE providers continuously update security **without IT intervention**, ensuring real-time protection.

✓ **Lower Infrastructure Costs** – Businesses **reduce CAPEX (capital expenditure)** by eliminating costly security appliances.

With **cloud-native security**, IT teams can focus on **strategic initiatives** instead of managing physical infrastructure.

4. Automating Security with AI and Machine Learning

The Limitations of Manual Security Management

Traditional security models **rely on manual processes** for:

- **Threat detection and response**
- **Traffic analysis and policy enforcement**
- **Incident investigation and remediation**

Manually managing security increases **the risk of human error**, delays threat responses, and **overburdens IT teams**.

How SASE Uses AI-Driven Automation

SASE leverages **AI and machine learning (ML) to automate security enforcement**. Key capabilities include:

✓ **Automated Threat Detection** – AI identifies and blocks threats **before they impact the network**.
✓ **Behavior-Based Anomaly Detection** – Machine learning models detect **unusual user activities and potential insider threats**.
✓ **Self-Healing Networks** – AI-powered systems **automatically adjust traffic routes** to avoid congestion and optimize performance.

By automating security processes, **SASE reduces manual workload, improves threat response times, and enhances security posture**.

5. Seamless Integration with Modern IT Environments

The Challenge of Integrating Legacy Security with Cloud Services

Many organizations struggle to integrate **traditional security solutions** with modern IT environments, such as:

- **Cloud applications (SaaS, IaaS, PaaS)**
- **Hybrid and multi-cloud infrastructures**
- **Remote and mobile workforces**

Traditional security tools **were not designed for the cloud** and often require **complex configurations** to secure cloud services.

How SASE Enables Seamless Integration

SASE is **built for cloud-first organizations**, offering:

✓ **Direct-to-Cloud Security** – Security services operate **at the cloud edge**, ensuring seamless integration with SaaS applications.

✓ **Multi-Cloud Support** – Protects data across **AWS, Azure, Google Cloud, and hybrid environments**.

✓ **Zero Trust Network Access (ZTNA)** – Ensures **secure access** to applications without requiring a VPN.

With SASE, IT teams **no longer need to retrofit legacy security tools** to work with modern cloud environments—it **seamlessly integrates with cloud and hybrid infrastructures**.

Conclusion: SASE Makes Network and Security Management Easier

SASE **redefines network and security management** by consolidating **multiple security solutions into a unified, cloud-based framework**. By doing so, it:

✓ **Eliminates the complexity of managing multiple security appliances**
✓ **Centralizes policy enforcement for consistent security across all environments**
✓ **Leverages AI-driven automation for threat detection and response**
✓ **Delivers cloud-native security that scales with business needs**
✓ **Simplifies IT operations, reducing manual workload and costs**

By adopting SASE, organizations can **significantly reduce operational complexity** while improving **security, scalability, and network performance**. As cyber threats evolve and cloud adoption increases, **SASE provides the agility and security modern enterprises need**. 🚀

Why SASE is Cost-Efficient and Future-Proof

Introduction: The Financial Burden of Traditional Network Security

In the rapidly evolving digital landscape, businesses must prioritize **cost efficiency and future-proofing** when designing their network security architecture. Traditional security models, built around **on-premise firewalls, VPNs, and physical appliances**, require **significant upfront investments** and ongoing maintenance, creating **high operational costs**.

Additionally, these legacy systems struggle to adapt to **cloud-based workloads, remote workforces, and modern cybersecurity threats**.

Secure Access Service Edge (**SASE**) is a **cost-effective, cloud-native** approach that eliminates **hardware dependencies, reduces IT complexity, and offers scalable security**. By converging **networking and security into a single platform**, SASE **lowers total cost of ownership (TCO) while ensuring long-term adaptability**.

1. Reducing Capital Expenditures (CAPEX) and Operational Costs (OPEX)

The High Cost of Traditional Security Infrastructure

Traditional security architectures depend heavily on **physical hardware**, such as:

- **Firewalls and intrusion prevention systems (IPS)**
- **VPN concentrators for remote access**
- **WAN optimization appliances**
- **Cloud security gateways and proxies**

These require **large upfront CAPEX investments**, plus **ongoing maintenance, upgrades, and replacements**, leading to high **operational expenses (OPEX)**. Moreover, as organizations expand, **scaling security requires additional hardware purchases**, further increasing costs.

How SASE Cuts Costs

SASE shifts security from **hardware-based solutions to a cloud-native model**, eliminating the need for **expensive on-premise appliances**. Key cost-saving benefits include:

✓ **No hardware purchases or upgrades** – SASE is delivered **as a cloud service**, eliminating the need for costly security appliances.

✓ **Lower maintenance and IT overhead** – Since security is managed in the cloud, IT teams **no longer have to maintain, patch, or upgrade hardware**.

✓ **Pay-as-you-grow pricing model** – Organizations only **pay for the security and network capacity they use**, allowing them to scale without overspending.

By moving to a **subscription-based, cloud-delivered model**, SASE **significantly reduces both CAPEX and OPEX**, making it a financially viable solution for businesses of all sizes.

2. Eliminating Redundant Security and Networking Tools

The Challenge of Managing Multiple Disparate Solutions

Organizations traditionally rely on **a patchwork of security and networking solutions** from multiple vendors, including:

- Firewalls
- Secure Web Gateways (SWG)
- Cloud Access Security Brokers (CASB)
- Zero Trust Network Access (ZTNA)
- Virtual Private Networks (VPNs)
- Software-Defined WAN (SD-WAN)

Each of these solutions requires **separate licenses, management interfaces, policies, and monitoring**, leading to:

✓ **Increased licensing costs** from multiple vendors

✓ **Higher IT workload** for managing different security products

✓ **Security gaps** due to inconsistent policy enforcement across tools

How SASE Consolidates Security and Reduces Costs

SASE **integrates multiple security and networking capabilities** into a **single cloud-based platform**, reducing the need for separate solutions. Benefits include:

✓ **Single vendor, single contract** – Businesses can consolidate security spending under **one provider**, reducing licensing costs.

✓ **Unified policy enforcement** – Security rules are **centrally managed and applied consistently** across all users, devices, and locations.

✓ **Lower IT administration costs** – Instead of managing multiple systems, IT teams work with **one centralized security platform**, saving time and resources.

By replacing **fragmented security stacks with an all-in-one solution**, SASE **streamlines security operations while cutting costs**.

3. Scalability Without the Cost of Expanding Infrastructure

The Scalability Challenge in Traditional Networks

As businesses grow and expand into **new locations, cloud environments, and remote workforces**, traditional security architectures **struggle to scale efficiently**. Challenges include:

- **Adding new branches requires deploying new security appliances**
- **Remote employees rely on inefficient VPNs, increasing infrastructure costs**
- **Cloud applications need additional security gateways**

Scaling these legacy solutions is **slow, costly, and resource-intensive**.

How SASE Enables Cost-Effective Scalability

SASE is designed for **seamless, on-demand scalability**, making it **ideal for growing organizations**. Benefits include:

✓ **Cloud-native scalability** – Businesses can scale security and networking **without purchasing additional hardware**.

✓ **Secure remote work without VPNs** – SASE uses **Zero Trust Network Access (ZTNA)** to provide **secure, direct-to-cloud** connectivity, eliminating VPN overhead.

✓ **Global reach without infrastructure expansion** – Cloud-delivered security extends **protection to any location or device**, without requiring new appliances.

Because SASE is **cloud-based and pay-as-you-go**, organizations can **expand their security coverage without significant upfront investment**.

4. Future-Proofing Against Evolving Cyber Threats

The Growing Complexity of Cybersecurity

Cyber threats are constantly evolving, and **legacy security solutions struggle to keep up**. Traditional networks **rely on static perimeter defenses**, which:

- **Lack visibility into cloud and remote traffic**
- **Require manual updates and patches** to address new threats
- **Struggle with real-time threat detection**

This outdated approach increases the risk of **data breaches, compliance violations, and costly security incidents**.

How SASE Future-Proofs Security

SASE is **built for modern security challenges**, leveraging **AI-driven threat detection, automated security updates, and Zero Trust principles** to provide:

✓ **Real-time protection against emerging threats** – SASE continuously updates security policies **without manual intervention**.

✓ **Adaptive security models** – AI-driven insights help **predict and prevent** cyberattacks.

✓ **Zero Trust architecture** – Verifies every user and device before granting access, **minimizing insider threats and unauthorized access**.

By providing **continuous protection with automatic updates**, SASE ensures organizations **stay ahead of new cyber threats without costly manual upgrades**.

5. Improved Network and Security Efficiency

The Performance and Cost Issues of Traditional Networks

Traditional network security models **route all traffic through central data centers** before reaching cloud applications, creating:

- **High latency and poor user experience**
- **Increased bandwidth costs due to unnecessary backhauling**
- **Performance bottlenecks at corporate firewalls and VPN gateways**

As more workloads move to the cloud, **this architecture becomes inefficient and expensive**.

How SASE Optimizes Network and Security Costs

SASE improves **network efficiency and cost-effectiveness** by:

✓ **Reducing bandwidth costs** – Traffic is routed **directly to cloud services** through **local SASE PoPs**, eliminating backhauling.

✓ **Optimizing performance with SD-WAN** – Dynamic path selection **improves network efficiency**, reducing reliance on costly MPLS links.

✓ **Lowering operational expenses** – Cloud-delivered security requires **less manual intervention**, reducing IT workload.

With **faster and more cost-effective traffic routing**, SASE **enhances both security and network performance while lowering expenses**.

Conclusion: SASE is a Smart Investment for Long-Term Cost Savings

Secure Access Service Edge (**SASE**) is a **cost-effective, future-proof security solution** that helps organizations **reduce expenses while improving security, scalability, and performance**. By:

✓ **Eliminating costly on-premise hardware**

✓ **Consolidating security and networking tools**

✓ **Providing seamless, scalable security coverage**

✓ **Automating threat detection and security updates**

✓ **Reducing bandwidth and network costs**

SASE **lowers total cost of ownership (TCO) and ensures long-term adaptability**. As **cyber threats evolve and businesses expand**, organizations that adopt SASE will benefit from a **more secure, flexible, and financially sustainable network security model**. 🚀

Implementation Considerations for SASE Adoption

Introduction: The Need for a Thoughtful SASE Implementation

Secure Access Service Edge (**SASE**) represents a transformative approach to networking and security, merging **SD-WAN, Zero Trust, cloud security, and AI-driven threat protection** into a single cloud-based architecture. However, successfully adopting SASE requires **strategic planning, proper execution, and alignment with an organization's existing IT infrastructure and security policies**.

Businesses must evaluate several key considerations, including **network architecture, security policies, user experience, and vendor selection**, to ensure a **seamless and effective transition to SASE**. Below are the **critical factors organizations should address** when implementing SASE.

1. Assessing Current Network and Security Infrastructure

Before migrating to SASE, organizations must **audit their existing network and security infrastructure**. This involves:

✓ Identifying **legacy network components** such as **firewalls, VPNs, MPLS connections, and data center security appliances**

✓ Mapping **traffic flow patterns**, including how users, devices, and applications interact across

on-premise, cloud, and remote environments

✓ Evaluating existing **security policies**, access controls, and **compliance requirements**

A thorough assessment helps organizations **pinpoint gaps, bottlenecks, and areas of improvement**, allowing for a **structured and phased approach to SASE implementation**.

2. Defining Clear Security and Compliance Requirements

Since SASE integrates **networking and security into a unified cloud-based solution**, businesses must define **clear security and compliance goals** before deployment. Key considerations include:

✓ **Zero Trust Network Access (ZTNA)** – Ensuring that only authenticated users and devices can access critical resources

✓ **Data Loss Prevention (DLP)** – Implementing policies to protect sensitive data from unauthorized access and leaks

✓ **Cloud security requirements** – Defining rules for securing cloud applications and **SaaS platforms**

✓ **Regulatory compliance** – Ensuring adherence to industry regulations such as **GDPR, HIPAA, PCI-DSS, and ISO 27001**

By establishing **strong security and compliance frameworks**, organizations can **avoid vulnerabilities and maintain regulatory adherence** throughout the SASE transition.

3. Choosing the Right SASE Vendor and Deployment Model

Not all SASE solutions are the same, and choosing the **right vendor** is crucial for a successful rollout. Organizations must consider:

✓ **Single-vendor vs. multi-vendor approach** – A **single-vendor SASE platform** ensures seamless integration, while a **multi-vendor approach** may provide greater customization.

✓ **Cloud-native vs. hybrid deployment** – Some organizations may prefer a **fully cloud-based SASE model**, while others require **hybrid deployments** that integrate on-premise security solutions.

✓ **Edge locations and Points of Presence (PoPs)** – Ensuring the SASE provider has **global coverage with PoPs close to users and applications** to reduce latency.

✓ **Integration with existing tools** – Checking whether the **SASE solution integrates smoothly with existing identity providers (IdP), endpoint security, and SIEM/SOAR platforms**.

Choosing a **vendor that aligns with business needs and future scalability goals** ensures a **successful SASE adoption**.

4. Transitioning from Legacy Network Models to SASE

A **gradual transition** is often the most effective way to implement SASE, as it **minimizes disruptions** and allows businesses to **test and optimize** their deployment. Steps for a smooth transition include:

✓ **Phased implementation approach** – Migrating specific locations, users, or applications to SASE in stages instead of all at once

✓ **Running parallel environments** – Allowing legacy systems to coexist temporarily with SASE to ensure continuity

✓ **Testing SD-WAN connectivity** – Optimizing SD-WAN configurations for better performance and **secure cloud access**

✓ **Deploying Zero Trust policies incrementally** – Gradually enforcing **Zero Trust authentication and access controls** across the network

A phased approach **reduces risk, improves adoption rates, and ensures a seamless transition** to a fully SASE-based architecture.

5. Ensuring User Experience and Performance Optimization

A common challenge during network transformations is maintaining **high performance and a seamless user experience**. SASE implementations should prioritize:

✓ **Optimized routing through SD-WAN** – Ensuring traffic takes the most efficient path to cloud applications

✓ **Minimizing latency through local PoPs** – Deploying **SASE Points of Presence (PoPs)** close to end users for faster response times

✓ **Implementing Secure Web Gateway (SWG)** – Filtering web traffic without slowing down performance

✓ **User-based policies for different access needs** – Assigning different security levels for **remote workers, branch offices, and on-premise users**

Proactively monitoring performance ensures that **network speed and security remain balanced**, providing **a better end-user experience**.

6. Training IT Teams and End Users on SASE Adoption

Successful SASE adoption depends on **effective training and change management**. Businesses should:

✓ **Educate IT teams on SASE architecture** – Providing hands-on training to manage, configure, and troubleshoot SASE components

✓ **Conduct security awareness programs** – Teaching employees about **Zero Trust principles, secure remote access, and phishing prevention**

✓ **Offer self-service portals for end-users** – Enabling employees to check their access logs and security status without IT intervention

✓ **Establish clear communication channels** – Keeping stakeholders informed throughout the transition process

By investing in training and awareness, businesses can **increase adoption rates and reduce resistance to change**.

7. Continuous Monitoring, Management, and Optimization

After deploying SASE, organizations must ensure **ongoing security monitoring, optimization, and compliance management**. Key actions include:

✓ **Real-time security analytics and threat detection** – Using **AI-driven threat intelligence** to detect anomalies and respond to security events

✓ **Regular performance assessments** – Monitoring **network performance, latency, and user experience** metrics

✓ **Policy updates and enforcement** – Continuously refining access policies to adapt to new security threats and business needs

✓ **Incident response planning** – Preparing for potential cyberattacks with **automated response playbooks**

Continuous monitoring ensures that **SASE remains effective, scalable, and aligned with evolving business and security needs**.

Conclusion: A Strategic Approach to SASE Implementation

Adopting **SASE is not just a technology shift—it's a fundamental change in how businesses approach networking and security**. To ensure a **successful and cost-effective implementation**, organizations must:

✓ **Assess current infrastructure and security gaps**

✓ **Define security, compliance, and performance goals**

✓ **Choose the right SASE vendor and deployment model**

✓ **Transition gradually from legacy networks to SASE**

✓ **Optimize performance for end users and cloud applications**

✓ **Train IT teams and employees for a smooth adoption process**

✓ **Continuously monitor and optimize SASE performance**

With **careful planning and execution**, businesses can **maximize the benefits of SASE**, achieving **stronger security, simplified network management, and improved cost efficiency for the future**. 🚀

Conclusion

The shift from **traditional network security** to **Secure Access Service Edge (SASE)** is more than just an upgrade—it's a **paradigm shift in how organizations protect their data, applications, and users** in an increasingly cloud-centric world. As businesses expand their remote workforce, adopt **multi-cloud environments**, and embrace **digital transformation**, legacy security models fail to provide the **agility, scalability, and comprehensive protection** needed to counter modern cyber threats.

SASE **converges networking and security** into a **cloud-delivered, unified framework**, eliminating the complexities of managing **disjointed security tools and rigid infrastructure**. With **Software-Defined WAN (SD-WAN), Zero Trust Network Access (ZTNA), Secure Web Gateway (SWG), Cloud Access Security Broker (CASB), Firewall-as-a-Service (FWaaS), and Data Loss Prevention (DLP)** integrated into one architecture, organizations can enforce **consistent security policies across all users, devices, and locations**—without compromising performance.

One of the **biggest advantages of SASE** is its ability to **enhance performance** while reducing costs. Unlike traditional security models that **backhaul traffic through centralized data centers**, SASE enables **direct, secure access to cloud applications** via globally distributed **Points of Presence (PoPs)**, reducing latency and **improving the end-user experience**. By leveraging **AI-driven threat intelligence and continuous monitoring**, organizations can **detect and mitigate security risks in real-time**, ensuring a **proactive rather than reactive** security approach.

Scalability and flexibility are at the core of SASE's value. In today's fast-paced digital landscape, businesses need solutions that can **adapt to evolving threats, compliance requirements, and workforce dynamics**. Traditional security infrastructures often **struggle with scalability**, requiring **expensive upgrades** and constant maintenance. With **SASE's cloud-native architecture**, organizations can easily scale security controls, **apply security policies dynamically**, and ensure seamless connectivity **without hardware dependencies**.

Despite its clear benefits, the **implementation of SASE requires careful planning**. Organizations must assess their **existing network architecture, security policies, and user** access requirements before transitioning. A **phased approach to SASE adoption**—starting with high-priority applications, remote users, and branch offices—can help minimize disruption and ensure a **smooth migration from legacy systems**. Proper **training for IT teams and end-users**, along with **continuous security monitoring and policy refinement**, will further strengthen the **effectiveness of SASE deployment**.

As cyber threats continue to evolve, **SASE represents the future of network security**, offering a **holistic, scalable, and cost-effective solution** for protecting **data, users, and applications in a cloud-first world**. Organizations that **embrace SASE today** will be well-positioned to **enhance security, improve operational efficiency, and future-proof their network infrastructures** for years to come. **The time to upgrade is now.** 🚀

Glossary

A

Access Control – A security technique that regulates who or what can view or use resources in a computing environment.

Artificial Intelligence (AI) in Security – The use of machine learning and AI-driven analytics to detect, prevent, and respond to cyber threats.

Attack Surface – The sum of all potential vulnerabilities and entry points through which an attacker can exploit a network or system.

B

Backhauling – The practice of routing all network traffic through a central data center for security inspection, often leading to performance degradation.

Bandwidth Optimization – The process of managing and optimizing network bandwidth to enhance performance and reduce latency.

C

Cloud Access Security Broker (CASB) – A security solution that provides visibility and control over cloud applications, enforcing security policies and protecting sensitive data.

Cloud Computing – The delivery of computing services (e.g., storage, processing, and networking) over the internet instead of local servers or personal devices.

Cloud-Delivered Firewall as a Service (FWaaS) – A cloud-based firewall solution that offers scalable security without the need for on-premises firewall appliances.

Compliance – Adherence to industry and government regulations regarding cybersecurity and data protection.

D

Data Center – A centralized facility used for computing, networking, and data storage, often housing critical IT infrastructure.

Data Loss Prevention (DLP) – A set of security tools and policies designed to prevent unauthorized access, sharing, or leakage of sensitive data.

Distributed Denial of Service (DDoS) Attack – A cyberattack in which multiple systems overwhelm a target's network or service with a flood of internet traffic.

E

Edge Computing – A computing model that processes data closer to its source rather than relying solely on centralized cloud or data centers, improving response times.

Encryption – The process of converting data into a coded format to prevent unauthorized access.

F

Firewall – A network security device or software that monitors and filters incoming and outgoing traffic based on predetermined security rules.

Firewall as a Service (FWaaS) – A cloud-based security solution that provides firewall functionality without requiring physical hardware.

I

Intrusion Prevention System (IPS) – A security tool that actively monitors network traffic for malicious activities and takes action to prevent attacks.

Identity and Access Management (IAM) – A framework for ensuring that only authorized users have access to specific resources.

Implicit Trust – A security weakness where a system assumes all internal network users are trustworthy, which can lead to vulnerabilities.

L

Latency – The delay in data transmission over a network, often affecting performance and user experience.

M

Malware – Malicious software designed to harm, exploit, or compromise computer systems and networks.

Multi-Cloud Strategy – The use of multiple cloud service providers to enhance redundancy, flexibility, and security.

N

Network Perimeter – The boundary between an internal trusted network and external untrusted networks, traditionally secured by firewalls and other security measures.

Network Security – A set of technologies and policies designed to protect networks from cyber threats and unauthorized access.

Next-Generation Firewall (NGFW) – A modern firewall that includes advanced security features such as deep packet inspection, intrusion prevention, and application control.

P

Policy-Based Security – A security approach where access and protections are determined by predefined rules and policies.

Point of Presence (PoP) – A physical or virtual location where a network or service provider offers connectivity and security enforcement.

R

Remote Work Security – Security measures designed to protect corporate data and users working outside traditional office environments.

Role-Based Access Control (RBAC) – A security model that restricts access to resources based on a user's role within an organization.

S

Secure Access Service Edge (SASE) – A cloud-based security architecture that combines network and security functions into a unified framework to enhance protection and performance.

Secure Web Gateway (SWG) – A security solution that monitors and controls web traffic to prevent malicious threats, enforce policies, and block unauthorized access.

Software-Defined WAN (SD-WAN) – A virtualized network architecture that improves connectivity and security for branch offices and remote users by optimizing traffic routing.

Security as a Service (SECaaS) – A cloud-based model that provides security solutions such as firewalls, threat detection, and identity management as a service.

T

Threat Intelligence – The collection, analysis, and application of data related to potential cyber threats to improve security defenses.

Traffic Inspection – The process of analyzing network traffic for security threats, compliance violations, or policy enforcement.

V

Virtual Private Network (VPN) – A secure tunnel that encrypts internet traffic, allowing users to access private networks remotely.

W

Workforce Mobility – The ability of employees to work securely from various locations using cloud applications and remote access technologies.

This **glossary** provides a **clear reference** for readers to understand **key concepts** related to **SASE, cybersecurity, and modern network architectures**. Let me know if you'd like to add more terms! 🚀

Recommended Reading & Resources on SASE

For readers who want to dive deeper into **Secure Access Service Edge (SASE)** and related cybersecurity topics, here are some **recommended books, whitepapers, articles, and online courses**:

📚 Books

1. **"Securing the Cloud: Security Strategies for the Ubiquitous Data Center"** – Vic (J.R.) Winkler
    a. A comprehensive guide on cloud security concepts, including Zero Trust and network security transformations.
2. **"Zero Trust Networks: Building Secure Systems in Untrusted Networks"** – Evan Gilman & Doug Barth
    a. Explains the **Zero Trust security model**, which is a key component of SASE.
3. **"Network Security Essentials: Applications and Standards"** – William Stallings
    a. Covers fundamental **network security principles**, including VPNs, firewalls, and encryption.
4. **"Cloud Security Handbook: A Hands-on Guide to Securing Cloud Environments"** – Eyal Estrin
    a. Provides **practical strategies** for securing cloud infrastructure, which aligns with **SASE architecture**.
5. **"Mastering Palo Alto Networks"** – Tom Piens
    a. Explores **next-gen firewall technologies**, network security, and cloud security—key elements in SASE implementation.

📄 Whitepapers & Reports

6. **Gartner's "The Future of Network Security Is in the Cloud"** (2019)
   a. This **landmark report** introduced the **SASE framework** and explains why traditional security models are becoming obsolete.
7. **Cisco's "SASE: Secure Access Service Edge Explained"**
   a. A breakdown of **SASE architecture** and how businesses can transition to a cloud-first security model.
8. **Palo Alto Networks' "The Essential Guide to SASE"**
   a. A **detailed look at SASE** and how it integrates with **SD-WAN, Zero Trust, and CASB**.
9. **Zscaler's "SASE for Dummies"**
   a. A beginner-friendly guide explaining **how SASE simplifies network security and improves user experience**.
10. **NIST Special Publication 800-207: Zero Trust Architecture**
- The official **Zero Trust** framework from the **National Institute of Standards and Technology (NIST)**—a key foundation of **SASE**.

📰 Articles & Blogs

11. **"SASE vs. Traditional Network Security: Why It's Time to Upgrade"** – TechTarget
- A comparison of SASE and traditional security models, explaining why organizations need to shift to **cloud-first security**.
12. **"Why Zero Trust is Essential for SASE"** – Dark Reading
- Explores how **Zero Trust principles** play a critical role in **SASE security architecture**.
13. **"The Rise of SASE: Why Enterprises are Moving to Cloud-Delivered Security"** – NetworkWorld
- Analyzes industry trends and adoption rates of **SASE frameworks**.
14. **"How SD-WAN and SASE Work Together"** – SDxCentral
- Explains the relationship between **Software-Defined WAN (SD-WAN) and SASE**, including benefits for enterprises.
15. **"Top SASE Providers and How to Choose the Right One"** – Cybersecurity Insiders
- A market overview of **leading SASE vendors**, including Cisco, Palo Alto Networks, Zscaler, and Fortinet.

🎓 Online Courses & Certifications

16. **"SASE Fundamentals"** – Coursera (offered by Palo Alto Networks)
- A beginner-friendly introduction to **SASE architecture, Zero Trust, and SD-WAN**.
17. **"Cisco Secure Access Service Edge (SASE) Certification"** – **Cisco Learning Network**

- A professional certification for IT professionals implementing **SASE solutions**.
18.   **"SASE & Cloud Security Essentials" – Udemy**
- Covers **SASE fundamentals, SD-WAN, ZTNA, CASB, and Secure Web Gateways (SWG)**.
19.   **"Fortinet NSE 7 – SASE Security Certification"**
- A certification course focused on **SASE implementation using Fortinet's security solutions**.
20.   **"Zero Trust Security & SASE" – Pluralsight**
- A deep dive into **Zero Trust, SASE components, and cloud security best practices**.

🌐 Industry Resources & Vendor Documentation

21.   **Gartner Peer Insights: Secure Access Service Edge (SASE)**
- Read **customer reviews and industry ratings** of various SASE providers.
22.   **Cisco's SASE Resource Center**
- Official **Cisco documentation and webinars** on **SASE, SD-WAN, and Zero Trust security**.
23.   **Palo Alto Networks Prisma SASE**
- Detailed information on **Prisma SASE solutions** and how they integrate with **CASB, ZTNA, and SD-WAN**.
24.   **Zscaler SASE Knowledge Hub**
- Vendor insights into **SASE deployments, performance improvements, and security benefits**.
25.   **Fortinet SASE Learning Portal**
- Guides on implementing **SASE solutions with Fortinet's security products**.

Final Thoughts

These resources will help **security professionals, IT administrators, and business leaders** understand **SASE's benefits, implementation strategies, and real-world applications**. Whether you're just getting started or looking for **advanced insights**, these books, reports, and courses will provide **valuable knowledge** on the future of **cloud-delivered network security**. 🚀

Would you like me to add vendor-specific comparisons or industry case studies? 😊